LAUGH OFF

LAUGH OFF

THE COMEDY SHOWDOWN
BETWEEN

★ ★ ★   ★ ★ ★

REAL LIFE AND THE PROS

★ BOB FENSTER ★

**Andrews McMeel
Publishing**

Kansas City

05 06 07 08 09 RR2 10 9 8 7 6 5 4 3 2 1

ISBN-13: 978-0-7407-5468-5

ISBN-10: 0-7407-5468-8

Library of Congress Control Number: 2005924762

www.andrewsmcmeel.com

Design and illustration by Pete Lippincott

CONTENTS

PART 1

WAR OF THE LAUGHS

★ ★ ★ ★ ★ ★ ★ ★

Worried that a flu outbreak would spread to his singers, **Rudolf Bing**, manager of New York City's Metropolitan Opera Company, posted this warning backstage:

CONFINE YOUR KISSING TO THE IRRESISTIBLE.

In our search for laughs, we shall attempt to follow Bing's wise advice.

We will also never forget these words of comic wisdom from writer **Rita Mae Brown**: "Lead me not into temptation. I can find the way myself."

These ideas frame the challenge of this book: What's funnier—real life or the comedy turned out by the professionals?

Stand-up comics and writers get paid the big bucks, and the little ones, to be funny. But wacky things happen all the time to people who think they're just going about their own business.

Where do all the laughs come from? If we're lucky, they come at us from all directions.

Reality is the underdog in this hilarious competition because life isn't trying to be funny. It's just trying to get through another day.

The writers and the stand-ups make you laugh because if they don't, they'll have to face reality and get a real job. Being funny is a defense mechanism against driving a cab, waiting tables, or other forms of serious employment.

Yet life has one advantage over professional comics: It doesn't tell the same jokes night after night.

So let's take a look at how life stacks up against the pros. We'll let irresistible chuckling be the judge, keeping in mind that as long as you're laughing you're on the winning side.

Or as comic **Milton Berle** said, "Laughter is an instant vacation." And we need as many of those as we can get.

CHAPTER 1

THE MAN WHO BOUGHT THE RED SEA

AND OTHER FUNNY MONEY STORIES

Money has always been a source of great humor—unless, of course, you don't have any.

But let's assume you're fabulously wealthy. Fun, isn't it? Plus, you never have to do what you don't want to do ever again. And suddenly, spelling no longer counts. Just ask **George Hearst**.

IT'S A FUNNY LIFE

 George Hearst's offspring ruled a newspaper empire, but the patriarch made his fortune in Nevada silver mines in 1859.

Although illiterate, he used his wealth to become a California senator. When he was criticized for being uneducated, Hearst responded: "They say I spell *bird* b-u-r-d. If b-u-r-d doesn't spell *bird*, what in hell does it spell?"

 A wealthy collector once asked the artist **William Hogarth** to paint the *Destruction of the Pharaoh's Host in the Red Sea*. But he wouldn't agree to pay Hogarth the artist's full asking price.

When Hogarth couldn't bargain up the price of the commission, he dreamed up an artist's revenge—and turned in a canvas that was solid red. When the collector complained he wasn't getting what he'd asked for, Hogarth explained that the Israelites had all passed through the Red Sea and the Egyptians were all drowned in it.

 The vastly wealthy **Baron Rothschild** became even richer by winning a lottery. As a tip, he offered the poor merchant who sold him the winning ticket a choice of rewards: $12,000 in cash or $3,600 a year for the rest of the man's life.

The ticket seller took the $12,000. "With the kind of luck you Rothschilds have," he explained, "I wouldn't live another six months."

 Yogi Berra, the Yankee slugger who once said, "I didn't really say everything I said," had a warped view of most things, including money. "A nickel," he pointed out, "ain't worth a dime anymore."

A nineteenth-century clergyman was counseling a young farm boy recently arrived in the big city. The boy asked, "Is it possible to lead a good Christian life in the city on eighteen dollars a week?"

The reverend laughed. "At that rate, that's about all you can do."

Poet **Louis Untermeyer** once gave a lecture, then generously returned the group's check for his fee so they could use it for future club events. "And what will you use the money for?" he asked.

"To help us get better speakers," he was informed.

Joseph Kennedy had a vast fortune and political ambitions for his sons. But no matter how much he achieved, the opposition press always referred to his family as the Irish Kennedys—a subtle way of implying that despite wealth and influence, the Kennedys would only go so far in national politics.

"I was born here," Kennedy complained. "My children were born here. What the hell do I have to do to be an American?"

You think the rich have no problems? Consider this revelation from English author **Logan Pearsall Smith**: "It is the wretchedness of being rich that you have to live with rich people."

When he was a poor writer, **Honoré de Balzac** had his fortunes suddenly reversed when a wealthy uncle died, leaving him enough money to pursue a career in writing.

Balzac sent a note to reassure his creditors: "Yesterday, my uncle and I passed on to a better life."

 When writer **John Steinbeck** and his wife, Carol, were touring Mexico, they stopped in a village market to look at the handicrafts.

Taking a liking to a piece of pottery, Carol bargained with the woman running the stall. "I would like to buy this, but I'm not rich."

The market woman closed the sale by responding, "You have shoes and a hat. Of course you are rich."

 Baseball slugger **Reggie Jackson** was one of the highest-paid athletes of his time. Jackson set trends so that the more money he commanded, the higher the salaries that lesser players were able to negotiate. According to Jackson, that was just about everyone else.

But Jackson's appreciation of his own uniqueness extended beyond baseball to capture the feeling of every kid who ever dreamed of stepping up to the plate in a major-league stadium.

"In the building I live in on Park Avenue, there are ten people who could buy the Yankees," he admitted. "But none of them could hit the ball out of Yankee Stadium."

If you've got it, flaunt it. That's the popular approach taken by many of the wealthy practitioners of pop music. But few rock stars have flaunted it like **Marie de' Medici**, the seventeenth-century queen of France. She once had a ballgown into which were sewn thirty-nine thousand pearls and three thousand diamonds. She wore it once, then had a maid throw it in the closet.

Tycoon **J. Paul Getty** was one of the richest men in the world, and he learned something from his wealth too. "Money isn't everything," Getty said. "But it sure keeps you in touch with your children."

What would you do faced with this tricky situation? When a British woman's wealthy husband died, he left her a large inheritance under one condition—to make up for her constantly nagging about his smoking, she had to smoke five cigars a day to claim the money.

Keith Moon of the rock band the Who was a leading proponent of trashing hotel rooms while the band was on tour. When he destroyed his first suite, his stunt was seen as an act of rock 'n' roll rebellion. Then it became a band signature. Then it became an obsession. Finally, it turned into a flamboyant way of getting rid of excess money.

Estimates are that during his career, Moon spent half a million dollars paying off hotels for all the damage he caused.

Many of us enjoy a good prank—especially if it's played on someone else. But you have to be rich to arrange this kind of joke with hotel management. The boys in the band **Fleetwood Mac** decided to play a prank on their manager while staying at England's prestigious St. James Hotel.

While he was out one night, they turned his room into a chicken coop, stuffing it with bales of hay, then tossing in fifty hens and roosters.

After the chickens covered everything in the hotel room with what chickens do, the band members herded the birds into the elevator and hit the lobby button. Then they rode down in another car to pay the bill.

Luxury hotels around the world have two types of reaction to destructive rock bands and other prank-inclined guests:

1. Get rid of the troublemakers.

2. Welcome the troublemakers. A hotel can earn a lot of money from the extra charges they'll run paying for all the havoc they cause.

 Asked about giving gifts that would be welcomed by the recipient, newspaper magnate **William Randolph Hearst** responded, "Money is appropriate, and one size fits all."

BONUS LAUGH
SUPPORT YOUR LOCAL PRESIDENT

Let's say the president of the United States knocks on your door and says, "We need the rest of your money. Quick."

The vice president in charge of collections then explains that there are countries waiting for us to blow them up so we can spend billions rebuilding them and they can be happy again and remember how important it is to always love your Uncle Sam.

Then he orders Secret Service agents to go through your cookie jar to find the last of your discretionary income. Instead, they find cookies, and they're stale.

At which point FBI agents inform you that you are in violation of the federal Foreign Cookie Registration Act, which requires you to have what the federal government wants when it wants it or back you go to whatever foreign land you might have come from.

If you didn't come from a foreign country, then the president is entitled to send you to the hot spot of his choice, where you must serve the government by searching for oil for an enlistment term of four to six years, whichever comes first.

Sorry, must have been dreaming.

FROM THE JOKE FILE

As three students are about to graduate from the seminary, an angel appears to them and says, "You three have been so good that we will grant you a gift. You may each choose wealth, wisdom, or beauty."

The first male student says, "I will take wealth, because if I'm rich enough I can hire learned men to advise me and beautiful women will love me for my money."

The second student, a woman, decides to take beauty. "Money always follows beauty," she reasons, "as does happiness. And if I'm happy and have enough money, I won't care about wisdom."

The third student thinks for a long time, then decides to take wisdom. The angel smiles at him, and the man is driven to his knees in a flash of understanding.

"Are you all right?" the other students ask him.

"Yes," the man says, nodding wisely. "But now I know I should have taken the money."

WHAT THE PROS SAY

 Comic **Rita Rudner:** "Some people get so rich they lose all respect for humanity. That's how rich I want to be."

 Comic **Steven Wright:** "Borrow money from pessimists. They don't expect it back."

Playwright **Jean Kerr:** "You don't seem to realize that a poor person who is unhappy is in a better position than a rich person who is unhappy. Because the poor person has hope. He thinks money would help."

Comic **Joe E. Lewis:** "It doesn't matter whether you are rich or poor, as long as you've got money."

Comic **W. C. Fields:** "A rich man is nothing but a poor man with money."

Comic **Milton Berle:** "Poverty is not a disgrace, but it's terribly inconvenient."

Comic **Jackie Mason:** "I have enough money to last me the rest of my life, unless I buy something."

Writer **Mark Twain:** "Buy land. They've stopped making it."

Writer **Dorothy Parker:** "If you want to know what God thinks of money, just look at the people He gave it to."

Comic **Spike Milligan:** "Money couldn't buy friends, but you get a better class of enemy."

Comic **Emo Philips:** "I was walking down Fifth Avenue today and I found a wallet. I was going to keep it, rather than return it, but I thought: Well, if I lost a hundred and fifty dollars, how would I feel? And I realized I would want to be taught a lesson."

Writer **Artemus Ward:** "Let us all be happy and live within our means, even if we have to borrow the money to do it with."

 Writer **P. J. O'Rourke:** "A record number of savings and loan failures left America with a nationwide shortage of flimsy toaster ovens, cheap pocket calculators, and ugly dinnerware."

 Comic **Henny Youngman:** "What's the use of happiness? It can't buy you money."

 Writer **Sholom Aleichem:** "The rich swell up with pride, the poor from hunger."

 Writer **Fran Lebowitz:** "Generally speaking, the poorer person summers where he winters."

 Journalist **Walter Bagehot:** "Poverty is an anomaly to rich people. It is very difficult to make out why people who want dinner do not ring the bell."

 Comic **Steve Martin:** "How to make a million dollars: First, get a million dollars."

 Writer **Kim Hubbard:** "One good thing about inflation is that the fellow who forgets his change nowadays doesn't lose half as much as he used to."

 Comic **Milton Berle:** "A man is hit by a car while crossing a Beverly Hills street. A woman rushes to him and cradles his head in her lap, asking, 'Are you comfortable?' The man answers, 'I make a nice living.'"

Comic **Tommy Cooper:** "I inherited a painting and a violin which turned out to be a Rembrandt and a Stradivarius. Unfortunately, Rembrandt made lousy violins and Stradivarius was a terrible painter."

MY TURN
BEYOND PRODUCT PLACEMENT

Hollywood could realize vast new fortunes, which the studio execs could stack on top of their vast old fortunes, if they took product placement in movies one step further and turned movies into products, like these:

1. *Wag the Dog Food.* How do we keep prices so low? We don't actually put anything in the can. We just pretend that we do.

2. *Nike of the Hunted.* The running shoe made especially for psychotic preachers. The shoe you'll love on one foot, hate on the other.

3. *Runaway Bride Perfume.* The only Julia Roberts–tested essence that attracts men you shouldn't marry, and neither should she.

4. *Twelve Angry Mentos.* The breath mint judged most effective by the district attorney's office.

5. *Last Tango in Paris Dance School.* Just because you're morbidly depressed doesn't mean you can't learn to dance the night away.

6. *Butch Cassidy and the Sundance Kid Film Festival.* Movies starring, directed, or laughed at by Robert Redford.

CHAPTER 2

SIT, MR. MAYOR, SIT

ON-THE-JOB LAUGHS 9 TO 4:55

You go to work and Coworker Johnson says, "Hello, Bigby." This makes you suspicious since your name isn't Bigby. Is Johnson trying to steal the promotion you deserve? What if you knew that Johnson was wearing women's underwear? Now that's funny. But what if Johnson was a woman? Really funny. A woman wearing women's underwear—didn't expect that, did you?

By now, while you're busy figuring out whether you should laugh or not, Johnson has become the boss, and her main job is to make your life as miserable as you thought it would be if she ever became boss.

Funny? Who's to say? Not you, obviously. You didn't get the promotion.

IT'S A FUNNY LIFE

 Is there a worse job than being roadie to a rock star? Sorting out all those green M&M's, dousing the star's feet with Perrier after concerts, constantly reassuring the idol that he's not losing his voice, his hair, his sanity?

Yes, one. How about being PR hack to a former rock star when he gets elected mayor of Palm Springs?

That would be **Marilyn Baker**, who was hired to help **Sonny Bono** deal with the rigors of his elected post in 1988. Among her duties: providing the new mayor with the cue cards Sonny needed to carry out his official responsibilities.

According to Baker, "For call to order, I wrote, 'Sit.' For salute the flag, I wrote, 'Stand up, face flag, mouth words.' For roll call, I wrote, 'When you hear your name, say yes.'"

Three months into Sonny's term as mayor, Baker quit.

 While shopping in a jewelry store, philosophy professor **Mortimer Adler** was asked by the store owner, "What do you do, Mr. Adler?"

"I'm a philosopher," Adler replied.

"No," the jeweler corrected him, "I meant, what do you do for a living?"

 When playwright **George S. Kaufman** arrived at a Broadway theater for a rehearsal, a newly hired stage-hand stopped him and asked if he was with the play.

"Let's put it this way," Kaufman replied, "I'm not against it."

MGM boss **Samuel Goldwyn** was complaining about the mountains of paperwork stacking up in the movie studio offices. He told an assistant, "I want you to throw everything out. But make a copy of everything first."

And that's why offices overflow with forgotten paper.

Berta Scharrer was a German biological researcher in the 1930s. Dr. Scharrer escaped from Nazi Germany with her husband, Ernst, also a biologist.

When they came to the United States, he was able to get research jobs at universities, but she could not. College science departments wouldn't hire a woman. So she continued her research, working for free.

Berta finally got a job in 1940 at Case Western University as a science instructor. But the job came with two conditions: She wasn't paid, and at departmental meetings she had to make the tea.

When actor **Richard Burton** was filming *The Assassination of Trotsky,* the French actor **Alain Delon** narrowly missed hitting him with an ax. Burton advised more caution in ax handling.

"There are plenty of French actors around," he told Delon. "But if you kill me, there goes one-sixth of all the Welsh actors in the world."

John Wanamaker was the first department store owner to commit to a major newspaper advertising campaign to attract and keep customers. Even after his ad campaign proved a big success, Wanamaker grumbled about the expense.

"Half the money I spend on advertising is wasted," he said. "Unfortunately, I can never figure out which half."

Most newspapers and magazines give away free copies to prominent people. The *Paris [Texas] News* once sent this note to the people on its comp list: "Because of increased costs, this publication comes to you twice as free as it used to be."

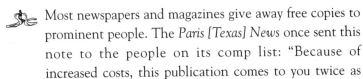

A businessman bragged to newspaper editor **Horace Greeley** that he was a self-made man. "That relieves God of a terrible responsibility," Greeley commented.

In 1975 the mayor of New York City received an offer from the Tigua Indians of Texas to buy back the island of Manhattan for the original price of twenty-four dollars in trinkets.

The offer came with one string attached: The Tiguas wanted the island returned to its original condition first. Before the mayor could hand over the keys to the city, he'd have to remove all the buildings.

Arthur Brisbane was an editorial columnist who spent fifty years working for the Hearst newspapers. As a reward for his service, the publisher offered Brisbane six months off with pay.

Brisbane turned down his publisher's generous offer, explaining: "The first reason is that if I quit writing my column for six months it might affect the circulation of your newspaper. The second reason is that it might not affect the circulation."

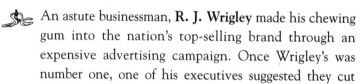

An astute businessman, **R. J. Wrigley** made his chewing gum into the nation's top-selling brand through an expensive advertising campaign. Once Wrigley's was number one, one of his executives suggested they cut back on their advertising. The boss refused.

"We'll keep advertising for the same reason a pilot keeps his engines running even when the plane is already in the air," he explained.

When a reader complained he had found a spider inside his newspaper, editor **Mark Twain** sent him a non-apology: "The spider was looking over our paper to see which merchant is not advertising so that he can go to that store, spin his web across the door, and lead a life of undisturbed peace ever afterward."

Arthur C. Clarke, who wrote the science fiction novel *2001: A Space Odyssey*, was also a scientist. He received a telegram from newspaper publisher **William Randolph Hearst** demanding, "Is there life on Mars? Cable one thousand words."

Clarke wired back: "Nobody knows. Repeat five hundred times."

 Every office manager complains about the mountains of paperwork they're stuck behind. But all they can do about the problem is file their complaints in triplicate.

Harold Alexander, a British minister of defense who had served in the army during World War II, came up with a unique system of reducing paperwork. At the end of each workday, he would take whatever papers, forms, and reports he hadn't gotten to and move them, unread, from his In basket to his Out basket.

When an aide asked why he did that, Alexander shrugged. "You'd be surprised how little of it comes back."

There is hope for bureaucracy yet.

 Would-be reporter **Irvin Cobb** figured his chances were slim for landing a job at the *New York Post*. So he decided to take the "let's stand out from the crowd or go down in flames" approach and sent this letter of application to the newspaper's editor:

"Unless you grab me right away, I will go elsewhere and leave your paper flat on its back right here in the middle of a hard summer, and your whole life hereafter will be one vast surging regret. The line forms on the right. Applications considered in the order in which they are received. Triflers and professional flirts save stamps. Write, wire, or call at the above address."

Got the job too.

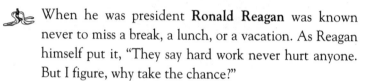 When he was president **Ronald Reagan** was known never to miss a break, a lunch, or a vacation. As Reagan himself put it, "They say hard work never hurt anyone. But I figure, why take the chance?"

Athletic movie star **Douglas Fairbanks** loved to do his own stunt work. But when filming *Robin Hood,* he was talked out of attempting a particularly dangerous stunt—climbing the chains of a drawbridge to get into a castle.

The stuntman who performed the feat looked clumsy on film. So the director decided to reshoot the scene the next day using another stuntman.

The new guy looked great climbing the chains. At the top of the wall, the stuntman turned around and waved, revealing himself to be Douglas Fairbanks.

Hollywood is not your typical corporation, but pin-stripers everywhere could learn a few management lessons from former MGM head **Sam Goldwyn**.

When approached by a subordinate with a good idea he wasn't interested in, Goldwyn turned him down, saying, "You are partly 100 percent right."

Aren't we all?

BONUS LAUGH
HOW TO SUCCEED IN BUSINESS WHILE REALLY LAUGHING

Brains sometimes work. Hard work? Luck? Could help. Or you could follow the advice of these people who laughed in the face of success (although usually after they'd had it).

★ Writer **Christopher Buckley:** "I vividly remember the speaker at my own graduation, so many years ago now. He or she said to us, 'You stand on the shoulders of people who came before you, so don't jiggle.'"

★ Baseball player **Jerry Coleman:** "Never ask why you've been fired because if you do, they're liable to tell you."

★ Writer **Cynthia Heimel:** "Stop listening to a society which tells you you're powerful when in fact a couple of rich guys control everything. Stop listening to beer commercials which instruct you to be a moron."

★ TV comic **Catherine O'Hara:** "Nighttime is really the best time to work. All the ideas are there to be yours because everyone else is asleep."

★ Writer **Dr. Seuss:** "Be who you are and say what you feel, because those who mind don't matter and those who matter don't mind."

☆ Monty Python's **Eric Idle:** "Bear in mind the simple rule: X squared to the power of two minus five over seven-point-eight-three times nineteen is approximately equal to the cube root of MCC squared divided by X minus a quarter of a third percent. Keep that in mind, and you can't go very far wrong."

☆ Writer **Mark Twain:** "Never put off until tomorrow what you can do the day after tomorrow."

FROM THE JOKE FILE

1. It was only Lisa's second day on the job, but she showed up an hour late. "You should have been here at nine," the manager said.

   "Why?" Lisa asked. "What happened then?"

2. When the corporate CEO died, Saint Peter met him at the Pearly Gates. "You have two options," Saint Peter told him, "Heaven or hell. Best procedure is to spend a day in each, then decide where you want to remain for eternity."

   The CEO went down to hell and was surprised to find a stunning country club with an Olympic swimming pool, a perfect golf course, and his company's board of directors waiting for him.

   They greeted him happily, and he spent the day swimming and playing golf, followed by drinks and a five-star meal. After dinner, he met Satan himself, who talked about how most people had the wrong idea of hell and how he hoped the CEO decided to join them.

The CEO spent the next day in heaven, where he received his first harp lesson and was given a Bible to read as an instructional manual.

Finally, Saint Peter said, "Time to make your eternal choice—heaven or hell."

The CEO made an executive decision. "Heaven is just what I expected," he said. "But let's face it, you can't compete with hell. Good-bye."

Saint Peter nodded, looking disappointed. But the CEO rushed down to hell, where he found a vista of fire and brimstone, with the board of directors and everyone else writhing in agony.

"I don't get it," the CEO said to Satan. "Yesterday, this place was perfect. But today, it's . . . hell."

Satan shrugged and said, "Yesterday, we were recruiting you. Today, you're staff."

3. "Why'd you transfer from the L.A. office to New York?"
   "So I could get paid three hours earlier."

4. The district manager stopped off at the sales office and asked the supervisor, "Exactly how many people work in this office?"
   The supervisor looked around the room and said, "Almost half of them."

WHAT THE PROS SAY

 Poet **Robert Frost:** "The world is full of willing people. Some willing to work. The rest willing to let them."

 Screenwriter **William Goldman:** "They should consider giving Oscars for meetings: Best Meeting of the Year, Best Supporting Meeting, Best Meeting Based on Material from Another Meeting."

 Poet **Ogden Nash:** "If you don't want to work, you have to work to earn enough money so that you won't have to work."

 Comic **Joey Adams:** "People are still willing to do an honest day's work. The trouble is they want a week's pay for it."

 Comic **Ellen DeGeneres:** "'Have a nice day.' Cashiers and other service-industry people are forced by their supervisors to say this to every customer. The cashiers don't mean it. What they're really saying is, 'Please, God, I don't want to get fired.'"

 Comic **Jerry Seinfeld:** "I don't know what it takes to get a cab driver's license. I think all you need is a face. This seems to be their big qualification."

 Comic **Steven Wright:** "Hard work pays off in the future. Laziness pays off now."

Comic **Fred Allen:** "A committee is a group of men who individually can do nothing but as a group decide that nothing can be done."

 Comic **Milton Berle:** "A committee is a group that keeps the minutes and loses hours."

 Poet **Robert Frost:** "The reason why worry kills more people than work is that more people worry than work."

 Comic **Steven Wright:** "Many people quit looking for work when they find a job."

 Writer **Jerome K. Jerome:** "I like work. It fascinates me. I can sit and look at it for hours."

 Comic **Robin Harris:** "I've been out of work so long, I forgot what kind of work I'm out of."

 Comic **Dennis Miller:** "If you get to thirty-five and your job still involves wearing a name tag, you've probably made a serious vocational error."

 Writer **Josephine Humphreys:** "In real estate it is part of the business to know of impending divorce and disease, the harbingers of real estate transactions."

 Comic **Milton Berle:** "A young man fills out an application for a job and does well until he gets to the last question, 'Who should we notify in case of an accident?' He mulls it over and then writes, 'Anybody in sight!'"

Comic **Steve Martin:** "I've got to keep breathing. It'll be my worst business mistake if I don't."

 Comic **Jerry Seinfeld:** "Why does that pharmacist have to be two and a half feet higher than everybody else? Who the hell is this guy? 'Clear out everybody, I'm working with pills up here. I can't be down on the floor with you people! I'm taking pills from this big bottle and then I'm gonna put them in a little bottle! And then I gotta type out on a little piece of paper! It's really hard.'"

MY TURN
THE MOST IMPORTANT JOB IN AMERICA?

Got to be president of the United States, doesn't it? That's what they keep telling us when they insist we choose between the lesser of two evils and the other lesser of two evils.

Yet for such an important job, there aren't many job qualifications. No intelligence test, obviously. No skills test. No psychological profile.

Lawyers have to pass bar exams. Doctors have to prove they know what they're doing before they get their license. Secretaries have to take typing tests. Presidents? Nothing.

Any American, rich or poor, can become president—as long as he's got $200 million for the campaign.

There's only one other job qualification: You have to look sincere while making campaign promises you have no intention of keeping, even if it were possible, which it isn't or someone would have kept one or two of them by now if just by accident.

You might say: But it doesn't take a rocket scientist to run the country. Well, shouldn't it? What if we had the smartest person running things instead of whichever one has the best ad agency?

CHAPTER 3

THE BORN-AGAIN PLAYBOY

REFLECTIONS ON LOOKING IN THE MIRROR

Magazine writer **Robert Benchley** once explained to a friend why he refused to look in mirrors: "Things are depressing enough as they are without my going out of my way to make myself miserable."

The rest of us may find out some funny things about ourselves and our pet egos when we look into the mirror.

IT'S A FUNNY LIFE

 Ever think about how happy you'd be if only you were rich and famous? Or just rich? Or even really, really close to rich? You'd never have to clean the bathroom again, and top-class lovers would be in persistent pursuit of your top-class butt.

But from the outside, we don't see the inner torment of the top pop celebrity—the anguish, the doubt every time she looks in the mirror and sees the horror of it all.

Let's have our pop goddess explain it herself: "When I was younger, I was never really insecure. Now I sometimes get insecure because people expect celebrities to look a certain way. And there are mornings I wake up and my butt feels fat."

Who suffered from the shame of the early-morning imagined fat butt? At the age of nineteen when she was number one on the charts, in the posters, and in the green eyes of much of our envious country? That would be **Britney Spears**.

 We already know you were **Cleopatra** in a former life because who wasn't? But if you could plan ahead to come back as anyone you wanted in your next life, who would you be?

One famous person has his next life neatly lined up. Can you guess who said "When I die, I would like to be born again as me"?

That would be Mr. *Playboy* magazine, **Hugh Hefner**.

To make the survey complete, we should find out what all the Playboy bunnies would like to come back as.

 When President **George W. Bush** returned to speak at the Yale commencement in 2001, he told the gathered students, "To those of you who received honors, awards, and distinctions, I say well done. And to the C students, I say you too can be president of the United States."

So let's see—all you need to become president is a C average. No problem there. Plus, a father who used to run the country and a couple hundred million bucks for advertising. That leaves me out, but it should cover most of the graduating class at Yale.

 Dr. Harold Urey won a Nobel Prize for chemistry but no awards for paying attention to details. One day while crossing the college campus where he worked, Urey stopped to talk to a colleague, then asked his friend, "Which way was I headed?"

"That way," said his associate, pointing.

"Good," Dr. Urey said, "then I've had my lunch."

Some millionaire athletes take themselves very seriously. Then there's basketball star **Charles Barkley**, who looked in the mirror and saw himself.

"My initial response was to sue her for defamation of character," Barkley said of one critic. "But then I realized that I had no character."

Charles Barkley would have gotten along with Yankee catcher **Yogi Berra**, who looked like what a catcher is supposed to look like—a beat-up old mitt.

But he didn't care. "So I'm ugly," Yogi said. "So what? I never saw anyone hit with his face."

When **Oliver Wendell Holmes Jr.** was a Supreme Court justice, Harvard Law School had a large portrait commissioned to hang in his honor in the school's library.

Upon the painting's completion, Holmes viewed the noble figure and confided in a friend, "That isn't me. But it's a damn good thing for people to think it is."

 Italian movie star **Marcello Mastroianni** took great pride in his appearance and wished Americans did the same. "I would shoot myself before letting myself get so fat," he said, referring to overweight Americans. "Your land of plenty is becoming a land of fat people."

 Chicago Bears linebacker **Dick Butkus** was a legend for his game face. To run in his direction was to prepare yourself for the onslaught of pain. But the football star didn't see himself the way his opponents did. "I'm not so mean," Butkus said. "I wouldn't ever go out to hurt anybody deliberately, unless it was, you know, important, like a league game or something."

 In Illinois **Abe Lincoln** was known as a good country lawyer who drew the short straw when it came to good looks.

One day while the future president was walking through town, a stranger pulled a pistol on him. "What quarrel do you have with me?" Lincoln asked the angry man.

Waving the gun at Lincoln, the stranger explained, "I swore myself an oath that if I ever met a man uglier than myself, I'd shoot him dead."

Lincoln looked the man over, then nodded. "Go ahead and shoot me, stranger," he said. "If I'm uglier than you, then I don't want to live."

A friend of the writer **Don Marquis** claimed to be descended from royalty, then asked, "And who are you descended from?"

"I am not a descendant," Marquis replied. "I am an ancestor."

A woman admirer was impressed when British Prime Minister **Winston Churchill** drew a large audience for one of his speeches. "It's quite flattering," he admitted. "But if instead of making a speech, I was being hanged, the crowd would be twice as large."

William Perry earned his nickname, the Refrigerator, with his size and appetite when he played the line for the Chicago Bears. How does a football player get to be that large? As Perry put it, "I've been big ever since I was little."

The poet **Eugene Field** told a story about why we so often find fault with each other. "An editor in Kankakee, falling in a burning passion with a vexatious rival, he wrote him a letter in this fashion: 'Sir, you are an ass, uncouth and rude, and will be one eternally.'"

Finishing the letter, the editor signed it: "Yours fraternally."

 Not many professional boxers see the value of a higher education. Heavyweight champ **George Foreman** explained it this way: "I think sleeping was my problem in school. If school had started at four in the afternoon, I'd be a college graduate today."

 The scientific genius **Albert Einstein** was traveling across the country by train. One evening in the dining car, Einstein realized he had forgotten his reading glasses and asked the waiter to read the menu for him.

"Sorry," the waiter whispered to the nuclear physicist, "but I can't read either."

BONUS LAUGH
WHAT THE STARS SAY
WHILE LOOKING IN THE MIRROR

☆ Movie star **Victor Mature:** "I'm not an actor, and I have sixty-four pictures to prove it."

☆ Movie star **Sean Connery:** "I've always hated that damn James Bond. I'd like to kill him."

☆ Singer **Bing Crosby:** "I think I've stretched a talent, which is so thin it's almost transparent, over quite an unbelievable term of years."

☆ Movie star **Julie Harris:** "Pictures make me look like a twelve-year-old boy who flunked his body-building course."

☆ Movie star **Maria Montez:** "When I look at myself, I am so beautiful I scream with joy."

☆ Movie star **Cary Grant:** "Everybody wants to be Cary Grant. Even I want to be Cary Grant."

☆ Movie star **Burt Reynolds:** "My movies were the kind they show in prisons and airplanes—because nobody can leave."

☆ Comic **Chris Rock:** "I'm not a superstar. Jim Carrey makes twenty million dollars a movie. I make a weird face when they tell me I have to pay eight-fifty to see one."

☆ TV comic **Lucille Ball:** "I'm not funny. What I am is brave."

☆ TV comic **Jack Benny:** "I don't deserve this award, but I have arthritis and I don't deserve that, either."

FROM THE JOKE FILE

1. As he grew up, Little Joe was often told the story about his uncles John and Saul, two devoutly religious men who both celebrated their twenty-first birthdays by walking on water.

When Joe turned twenty-one, he determined to prove his own spiritual worthiness by duplicating his uncles' feat. He had a friend row him in a boat into the middle of the lake.

"If my uncles did it, I can too," Joe said. Then he stepped over the side of the boat and sank. He would have drowned if his friend hadn't pulled him from the lake.

When he returned home ashamed of his failure, Joe asked his grandmother, "What's wrong with me? Why couldn't I walk on the water like Uncle John and Uncle Saul?"

His grandmother shook her head. "Saul and John were born in January, Joe. You were born in July."

2. Two idiots walk past a mirror. The first guy stops and says, "The face is familiar, but I can't quite remember the name."

The second idiot looks in the mirror and says, "You fool, it's me."

WHAT THE PROS SAY

 Nineteenth-century lecturer **Josh Billings:** "A dog is the only thing on earth that loves you more than you love yourself."

 Comic **Rodney Dangerfield:** "I found there was only one way to look thin—hang out with fat people."

 Comic **Spike Milligan:** "How long was I in the army? Five-foot-eleven."

Comic *Steven Wright:* "A lot of people are afraid of heights. Not me, I'm afraid of widths."

 Comic *Rodney Dangerfield:* "I told my psychiatrist that everyone hates me. He said I was being ridiculous, everyone hasn't met me yet."

 Writer *Jane Wagner:* "Delusions of grandeur make me feel a lot better about myself."

 Writer *Oscar Levant:* "I'm controversial. My friends either dislike me or hate me."

 Writer *Jane Wagner:* "The ability to delude yourself may be an important survival tool."

 Comic *Steven Wright:* "I was trying to daydream, but my mind kept wandering."

 Cartoonist *Doug Larson:* "The only nice thing about being imperfect is the joy it brings to others."

 Writer *Jane Wagner:* "I have gained and lost the same ten pounds so many times over and over again my cellulite must have déjà vu."

 Writer *Douglas Adams:* "One always overcompensates for disabilities. I'm thinking of having my entire body surgically removed."

 Writer *Rita Mae Brown:* "One of the keys to happiness is a bad memory."

Writer *Garrison Keillor:* "You don't want a fifty-dollar haircut on a fifty-cent head."

 Writer *Stephanie Brush:* "Therapy can replace the nagging suspicion that you are inadequate with a sense of absolute certainty that you are."

 Comic *Ellen DeGeneres:* "Some people believe that it's a good idea to face your fears. I usually feel that it's much healthier to tie them up in a bag, drive out to the country, chuck them out your window, then drive home as fast as you can."

 Comic *Dave Thomas:* "I don't exercise. What's in it for me? I view my body as a way of getting my head from one place to another."

 Writer *Rita Mae Brown:* "One out of every four Americans is suffering from some form of mental illness. Think of your three best friends. If they're okay, then it's you."

MY TURN
WHO'S THE FUNNIEST OF THEM ALL?

Let's say that you're two steps from the blues. Which way do you go now? If you run away from your problems, you're three steps from the blues—that's not so funny. You could go the other way, one step from the blues—kind of funny. But was B.

B. King ever one step from the blues? No, he went all the way. He was *into* the blues.

What if you suddenly ran off to Russia and said, "Look at me now. I'm only two steppes from the blues."

Funny? Sure, to a Russian. But remember, the Russian idea of humor is: Has the tsar stopped hammering nails in your head yet? No? Ha.

Americans expect more deliverables from their humor than vague references to Russian headache cures. They want to know that what they laugh at is a good reflection of who they are, how much money they earn, and how hot their date is.

That's why Americans spend more time looking in the mirror than anyone else in the world. They have so much more to look at.

CHAPTER 4

CAN LOVE GIVE ELVIS A BAD NAME?

ROMANTIC LAUGHS WITH MEN, WOMEN, AND OTHERS

"It isn't tying himself to one woman that a man dreads when he thinks of marrying," newspaper columnist **Helen Rowland** observed. "It's separating himself from all the others."

No separation in this book. Ladies, gentlemen, whatever—when the bell rings, have at it.

IT'S A FUNNY LIFE

 In 1947 **Milton Berle** was one of the biggest names in comedy. But as his career rose, his marriage failed, leading to a divorce from his wife **Joyce Mathews**.

Two years later, Berle and Mathews got married for the second time. Why marry the same woman all over again? "Because," Berle explained to reporters, "she reminds me of my first wife."

 General **Mark Clark** was in the thick of the action during World War II. He worked with some of the great military minds of his age, including Generals **Dwight Eisenhower** and **George Patton**.

When a reporter asked Clark for the best advice he'd ever received, the general replied, "To marry the girl I did."

"And who gave you that advice?" the reporter asked.

"She did," the general explained.

 Each year some 200,000 people come to Vegas to get married. Or they come to Vegas to try their luck and decide to get married while in the gambling mood.

Many of them go all the way to Graceland Chapel so they can be married by a minister who's also an Elvis impersonator.

In 2001 one of the Elvis ministers, **Kent Ripley**, was crying in the chapel when he told reporters, "They only do it for the bucks. I've even seen ministers dressed like this make a pass at a bride. It gets me upset. They're giving **Elvis** a bad name."

 Was comic **Roseanne Barr** bitter about her ex-husband? Not by Hollywood standards. "I'm not upset about my divorce from **Tom Arnold**," she explained. "I'm only upset I'm not a widow."

 Perhaps Roseanne should have listened to the wisdom of movie star **Shelley Winters**, who said, "In Hollywood all marriages are happy. It's trying to live together afterward that causes the problems."

 When he served on the Supreme Court, Justice **Felix Frankfurter** was asked by a friend to officiate at his wedding. Frankfurter had to turn him down, explaining that a Supreme Court justice did not have the authority to marry people.

His friend was surprised because any town judge in America had that authority. "Yes," Frankfurter acknowledged, "but marriage is not considered a federal offense."

 Movie actress **Ilka Chase** divorced actor **Louis Calhern** after they were married for only six months. When Calhern remarried, Ilka sent his new wife a box of her leftover calling cards engraved "Mrs. Louis Calhern."

Along with the gift came a note from Ilka: "Julia, hope these reach you in time."

 Movie stars tend to marry other movie stars, which may crush their fans but is really a favor to everyone they don't inflict their egos upon. When star **Fernando Lamas** asked star **Esther Williams** to marry him, he uttered that romantic cliché, "Let me take you away from all this."

"Away from all what?" Esther Williams said. "I'm a movie star!"

"Diamond" Jim Brady made a unique proposal of marriage to singer **Lillian Russell**. He sat her down in a chair, then placed $1 million in cash in her lap. She turned him down anyway.

Witty Hollywood hypochondriac **Oscar Levant** pointed out, "If **Judy Garland** and I had married, she would have given birth to a sleeping pill instead of a child. We could have named it Barb Iturate."

BONUS LAUGH
YOU DO, DO YOU?

Thinking of getting married? You might want to skip this section.

Comic **Rita Rudner:** "My boyfriend and I broke up. He wanted to get married and I didn't want him to."

Writer **Wilson Mizner:** "The days just prior to marriage are like a snappy introduction to a tedious book."

Playwright **Jean Kerr:** "Marrying a man is like buying something you've been admiring for a long time in a shop window. You may love it when you get it home, but it doesn't always go with everything else in the house."

Writer **Heywood Broun:** "The only real argument for marriage is that it remains the best method for getting acquainted."

Comic **Groucho Marx:** "I was married by a judge. I should have asked for a jury."

Comic **Jerry Seinfeld:** "I was best man at a wedding one time. I thought it was a little too much in the title there: best man. I think we ought to have the groom and a pretty good man. I mean, if I'm the best man, why is she marrying him?"

Comic **Bob Hope:** "You know marriage is making a big comeback. I know that in Hollywood people are marrying people they never married before."

Comic **Joey Adams:** "Marriage is give and take. You'd better give it to her or she'll take it anyway."

TV comic **Jack Benny:** "My wife, Mary, and I have been married for forty-seven years and not once have we had an argument serious enough to consider divorce. Murder, yes, but divorce, never."

Comic **Bob Hope:** "Everyone's getting married. I saw a car driving up the street with a pair of shoes hanging out the back. I said to the guide, 'Wedding?' He said, 'No, pedestrian.'"

Comic **Groucho Marx:** "Politics doesn't make strange bedfellows. Marriage does."

Writer **J. B. Priestley:** "Marriage is like paying an endless visit in your worst clothes."

Writer **H. L. Mencken:** "Marriage is a wonderful institution, but who would want to live in an institution?"

Comic **Alan King:** "He had one more standard question. They've always gotta ask it. It's part of the ritual. 'Will you support my daughter in the manner to which she's accustomed?'

'Sure,' I replied. 'We're moving in with you.'"

Writer **W. Somerset Maugham:** "Marriage is a very good thing, but I think it's a mistake to make a habit of it."

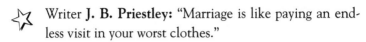

FROM THE JOKE FILE

1. "Today's my husband's birthday," a woman told her friend.
   "What are you getting for him?" her friend asked.
   "Make me an offer," the wife said.

2. A newspaper editor received this note from a reader: "My wife was about to file for a divorce when she read the article in your paper about the importance of giving second chances in making a marriage work. So she changed her mind about the divorce. Effective today, cancel my subscription to your paper."

3. Why does the bride wear white?
   Because it's good for the dishwasher to match the stove and refrigerator.

4. A dating service promised to match couples by their IQ ratings. A woman came in with an IQ of 170, and they matched her with a college professor. She was happy to find they shared interests in astrophysics, Greek history, and chess.

   The next woman had an IQ of 140, and they matched her with the CEO of a large corporation. Good match, as they were both interested in the Internet, French cuisine, and Japanese cinema.

   The third woman didn't think the dating service would be able to help her since she only had an IQ of 75. But the service introduced her to a man with an identical IQ of 75.

   "But what are we going to talk about?" she asked.

   The man shrugged and said, "Been to any hot auditions lately?"

5. Jeff's blind date with Suzanne went bad from the beginning. By the time they sat down for a drink, it was clear they were not hitting it off. Fortunately, Jeff had asked his friend Todd to phone him so he'd have an excuse to get out of the date if it didn't turn out well.

   When Todd called, Jeff listened to his cell phone in shock for a moment, then turned to Suzanne. "I have to leave," he said. "My aunt just died."

   "Thank God," Suzanne said. "If yours hadn't, mine would have had to."

WHAT THE PROS SAY

 Comic **Will Rogers:** "There are two theories to arguing with a woman. Neither one works."

 Comic **Henny Youngman:** "I've kissed so many women I can do it with my eyes closed."

 Comic **Rodney Dangerfield:** "My wife and I were happy for twenty years. Then we met."

 Comic **Jerry Seinfeld:** "We men know, no matter how poorly we behave, it seems we somehow end up with women anyway . . . Beautiful women—men are with them. Do you think these are special men? Gifted, highly unusual, one-of-a-kind men? These are the same jerks and idiots that I'm talking about . . . Men, as an organization, are getting more women than any other group working anywhere in the world today."

 Comic **Bob Hope:** "People who throw kisses are hopelessly lazy."

 Poet **Robert Frost:** "Love is an irresistible desire to be irresistibly desired."

 Comic **Homer Haynes:** "Love is the only game that will never be postponed on account of rain."

 The Simpsons creator **Matt Groening:** "Love is a snowmobile racing across the tundra and then suddenly it flips over, pinning you underneath. At night, the ice weasels come."

 Poet **Ogden Nash:** "A husband is a guy who tells you when you've got on too much lipstick."

 Comic **Jay Leno:** "Don't forget Mother's Day. Or as they call it in Beverly Hills, Dad's Third Wife Day."

 TV comic **Jack Benny:** "Give me golf clubs, fresh air, and a beautiful partner, and you can keep the clubs and the fresh air."

 Nineteenth-century lecturer **Josh Billings:** "Love is said to be blind, but I know some fellows in love who can see twice as much in their sweethearts as I do."

 Comic **Rodney Dangerfield:** "I haven't spoken to my wife in years. I didn't want to interrupt her."

 Comic **Phyllis Diller:** "Never go to bed mad. Stay up and fight."

 Writer **Dorothy Parker:** "Most good women are hidden treasures who are only safe because nobody looks for them."

 TV comic **Bill Maher:** "Women cannot complain about men anymore until they start getting better taste in them."

 Writer **Rita Mae Brown:** "My lesbianism is an act of Christian charity. All those women out there praying for a man, and I'm giving them my share."

Writer **Ring Lardner** (asked if his wife had helped his career): "She dusted my typewriter in 1922. Late one night in 1924 we got home from somewhere and I said I was hungry, and she gave me a verbal picture of the location of the pantry."

Comic **Rita Rudner:** "I love being married. It's so great to find that one special person you want to annoy for the rest of your life."

Movie comic **Groucho Marx:** "Alimony is like buying hay for a dead horse."

Comic **Rita Rudner:** "Whenever I date a guy, I think: Is this the man I want my children to spend their weekends with?"

Writer **Simone de Beauvoir:** "Why one man rather than another? It was odd. You find yourself involved with a fellow for life just because he was the one that you met when you were nineteen."

Writer **Cynthia Heimel:** "You know what we can be like: See a guy and think he's cute one minute. The next minute our brains have us married with kids. The following minute we see him having an extramarital affair. By the time someone says, 'I'd like you to meet Cecil,' we shout, 'You're late again with the child support!'"

Writer **H. L. Mencken:** "A man always remembers his first love with special tenderness, but after that he begins to bunch them."

Comic **Phyllis Diller:** "I always wondered how I could tell when the right one came along. But it was easy. He was the only one that came along."

 Writer **Nora Ephron:** "It's true that men who cry are sensitive to and in touch with feelings. But the only feelings they tend to be sensitive to and in touch with are their own."

 Newspaper columnist **Helen Rowland:** "There is no such thing as a confirmed bachelor in the countries where harems are fashionable."

 Writer **Jane Wagner:** "'But doesn't it kill romance?' you say. And I say, 'What doesn't?'"

 Writer **Edna O'Brien:** "People liking you or not liking you is an accident and is to do with them and not you. That goes for love too, only more so."

 Fashion columnist **Katharine Whitehorn:** "Whole nineteenth-century theories were based on the smaller size of the brain of women and 'inferior races'—until it was found that elephants' brains were even larger than men's."

 Writer **Helen Rowland:** "After a few years of marriage a man can look right at a woman without seeing her, and a woman can see right through a man without looking at him."

 Writer **George Bernard Shaw:** "Love is a gross exaggeration of the difference between one person and everybody else."

Writer **Helen Rowland:** "One man's folly is another man's wife."

 Comic **Ronnie Shakes:** "I wouldn't mind being the last man on earth, just to see if all those girls were telling me the truth."

 Comic **Bill Cosby:** "Maybe the best answer a husband can give to 'How was your day?' is 'I spent it dreading that question.'"

 Writer **Helen Rowland:** "When a man makes a woman his wife, it's the highest compliment he can pay her, and it's usually the last."

MY TURN
COMING TO A THEATER NEAR YOU: *THE GREATEST STORY NEVER TOLD*

PRODUCER: I love it, but the plot's all wrong. Where's the triangle? If it was *Adam and Eve and Suzie*, maybe.

WRITER: But *The Garden of Eden* is a classic. Good, evil, loss of innocence.

PRODUCER: Innocence is good. I'm all for losing it. But I can't make a movie where the big money shot is two people eating an apple. Now if they were tempted by the soft drink of forbidden knowledge, maybe. The product endorsements would cover my investment. Apples? There hasn't been an apple movie that's done box office since Snow White got the late-night munchies.

WRITER: But it's the greatest love story ever told. Well, the first.

PRODUCER: Boy meets girl. Boy loses paradise. Boy finds a life full of pain, hard work, and death. Kind of a downer, isn't it?

WRITER: How about *Big Adam and the Babe*, the untold story of two crazy kids who meet at Eden High, eat an American pie, and end up with twenty-five billion grandkids?

CHAPTER 5

A LITTLE MORE VIRGINITY

AND OTHER FUNNY TALES OF SHOWBIZ GLORY

Theater critic **George Jean Nathan** found that booze gave him the patience to sit through a lot of bad plays. Or as he explained his approach to the theater: "I only drink to make other people more interesting."

The drunks of show business are legendary, but so are the funny characters, the oddball performers, and other interesting showbiz people.

IT'S A FUNNY LIFE

 Why does one movie become a box office smash, while the next one flops? Is it the stars? The story? The million-dollar ad campaign, without which we wouldn't know this is the most exciting movie ever made since the one that opened last Friday?

Hollywood has made plenty of lousy $100 million movies that were huge box office hits, the ones that, when you see them two years later on TV, you go: What else is on?

Then there are the great movies that flopped at the box office. Or as MGM boss **Sam Goldwyn** explained it, "If people don't want to go to a picture, nobody can stop them."

 In 1924 playwright **George Bernard Shaw** sent **Winston Churchill** two free tickets to the opening night of his play *Saint Joan*, along with a note informing Churchill, who was then England's chancellor of the exchequer, that he should bring along a friend, "if you have one."

Unable to attend the opening, Churchill returned the tickets to Shaw but asked for seats to the play's second night, "if there is one."

 Opera singers are noted not only for their voices but also for how they perform the dramatic death scenes that occur so frequently in grand opera.

Two temperamental opera singers were rehearsing a duet in which the bass ended the scene with his dramatic expiration. Conductor **Sir Thomas Beecham** complained that the singers weren't getting the timing right. The soprano kept coming in late.

But she said it wasn't her fault—the bass was dying too soon.

"You are in error," Beecham assured her. "No opera singer has ever died half soon enough."

Movie mogul **Darryl Zanuck**, the head of Twentieth Century Fox, got into an argument with the caustic wit and sometime actor **Oscar Levant** when he made the mistake of asking Oscar his opinion of the studio's new film.

"I think the picture stinks," Levant replied.

Getting mad, Zanuck fumed, "Who the hell are you to think the picture stinks?"

Levant replied quite reasonably, "Who the hell do you have to be to think the picture stinks?"

Harry Cohn, who ran Columbia Studios in Hollywood's golden years, was not the easiest movie mogul to get along with. He once got mad at screenwriter **Jo Swerling** because Swerling's wife had dented Cohn's car in the studio parking lot.

Swerling shrugged it off, explaining, "She must have thought you were in it."

The violinist **Mischa Elman** went with his friend pianist **Josef Hofmann** to hear the debut recital by a young violinist, who turned out to be the future great **Jascha Heifetz**. At a break, Elman turned to his friend and commented, "Awfully hot in this auditorium, isn't it?"

Hofmann shook his head and said, "Not for pianists."

When the young **Gregory Peck** had his first success in movies, he went with a friend to celebrate at Manhattan's swanky Stork Club, but didn't get one of the tables the popular nightclub reserved for big celebrities.

"Tell them who you are," Peck's friend suggested.

Peck wouldn't do it. "If I have to tell them who I am," he said, "then I ain't."

 After classical violinist **Fritz Kreisler** was invited to a society party, the hostess urged, "Of course, you'll bring your violin."

"In that case," Kreisler said, "my performing fee is two thousand dollars."

Insulted (or caught out), the woman huffed, "In that case, I shall ask you not to mingle with my guests."

"In that case," Kreisler replied, "my fee will only be one thousand dollars."

 The English writer **Charles Lamb** sat in the audience when one of his plays opened in a London theater. Much to the playwright's unhappy surprise, the final curtain was met by a chorus of hisses from the displeased audience.

Thinking quickly, Lamb joined in the hisses so no one would mistake him for the author.

After recovering from that embarrassing ordeal, Lamb formed the Society of Damned Authors. To qualify for membership, a playwright needed one of his productions roundly booed by a paying audience.

The club's attitude toward theatergoers was, "The only legitimate end of writing for them is to pick their pockets and, that failing, we are at full liberty to vilify and abuse them as much as ever we think fit."

 The English actor **Ralph Richardson** realized halfway through the opening night of a new play that it wasn't going well. To the surprise of the rest of the cast, he suddenly stepped toward the footlights and called to the audience, "Is there a doctor in the house?"

One man in the audience acknowledged that he was a physician. "Doctor," the actor addressed him, "isn't this play awful?"

Got the only laugh of the night.

 Flamboyant movie star **Mae West** was notorious in Hollywood for stealing scenes from her costars. The accomplished Broadway actress **Alison Skipworth** ventured to costar with West in the movie *Night After Night*.

But after a day of filming, Skipworth got upset with West for upstaging her in front of the camera. "I'll have you know," Alison said huffily, "that I'm an actress."

Didn't faze Mae West a bit. She just laughed and told Skipworth, "It's all right. I'll keep your secret."

 When **Giulio Gatti-Casazza** ran New York City's Metropolitan Opera, he turned down a singer who had come to him from Italy's prestigious La Scala Opera.

The singer, furious at being rejected, told the director, "When I was with La Scala, they thought so much of my voice they insured it for fifty thousand pounds."

Gatti-Casazza was impressed but not moved. "And what did La Scala do with the money?" he asked.

 Late in her Hollywood career, **Jane Fonda** became more famous for her exercise videos than her movies. But not everyone went along with the Fonda workout program.

Singer and movie star **Dolly Parton** would have nothing to do with Fonda's aerobic dancing. Why not? "I'm funny about who I sweat with," Dolly explained.

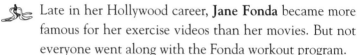 Actor **John Gielgud** was preparing to play Othello but couldn't grasp the power of jealousy that drove Shakespeare's avenger. He finally got an insight into jealousy's crippling grip when considering fellow actor **Laurence Olivier**.

"When Larry had a success as Hamlet, I wept," Gielgud said, and then he had a handle on Othello's emotional nature.

 You never want to give critics an opening because they'll always take it. When *Life* magazine movie critic **Robert Sherwood** got into an argument about cowboy movie stars, he wrote in reference to one oater, "They say he rides like part of the horse, but they don't say what part."

 Minimally dressed singer **Charo** liked to shake it up for her audiences in Las Vegas, and her fans appreciated the effort.

Charo had a unique way of expressing that relationship: "When I hear whistles," she said, "I get bumps all over my goose." This was undoubtedly as good for the gander.

French admirers of **Gioacchino Rossini** raised money to erect a statue of the composer. Rossini was shocked to learn that the statue would cost them ten million francs. He had a better idea. "For five million," he offered, "I'll stand on the pedestal myself."

Ava Gardner was an outspoken Hollywood star, even when it came to old friends like the glamorous **Lana Turner**, who went into seclusion late in her career.

"Lana thinks that absence will make the public's heart grow fonder," Ava observed. "All absence does is make people think you're dead."

Some movie directors get carried away with the search for the perfect shot. When **Sydney Pollack** directed *The Electric Horseman*, he reshot the big kiss between **Robert Redford** and **Jane Fonda** fifty times.

The film's accountant estimated that the single kiss cost the studio $300,000, commenting, "It would have been cheaper if Redford had kissed the horse."

When **Katharine Hepburn** and **John Barrymore** filmed *A Bill of Divorcement*, the two stars took a strong dislike to each other. As the movie wrapped, Hepburn turned to her male lead and said, "Thank goodness I don't have to act with you anymore."

Barrymore got the last word and the last laugh, replying, "I didn't know you had."

 Some movie directors sweet-talk their stars into giving the performances they want. Then there was director **Otto Preminger**, who was known in Hollywood for sneaking up behind nervous actors and screaming at them, "Relax!"

Actor **Sal Mineo** recalled, "Then he was angry and disappointed when, for some reason, that didn't relax you."

 Ralph Richardson was one of England's great classical actors, a star of the stage who also did a lot of screen work. But he suffered from no delusions about his craft. "Acting," he said, "is merely the art of keeping a large group of people from coughing."

 Tallulah Bankhead had a long career in the movies and on the stage. She worked hard to make sure she stayed a star as she grew into older roles.

Here's the advice she gave many a younger actress pushing her for parts: "If you really want to help the American theater, don't be an actress, darling. Be an audience."

 Seventeenth-century English playwright **Thomas Otway** was one of the original starving writers. He supported his meager career as an actor and playwright by begging in the streets. One morning, he begged enough money to buy himself a roll. He took one big bite of the roll, choked on it, and died.

Just another victim of show business.

 If you think the Miss America shows are getting rather dull, perhaps they could take a tip from the Miss Zambia contest. In 1972 the winner didn't walk off the stage with a college scholarship. She won a cow.

I don't know about you, but I'd watch the TV show again to see the look on the face of the newly crowned Miss America when they present her with her victory cow.

 Producer **George M. Cohan** sat in the theater auditioning a would-be actor. Cohan quickly interrupted the monologue and asked the actor to move farther upstage. "You're too close to the footlights," he explained.

The actor inched upstage then launched back into his audition when Cohan interrupted again, asking the actor to move even farther upstage.

"But if I go any farther back," the actor protested, "I'll be off the stage entirely."

"Now you've got the idea," Cohan called from the empty seats.

 When comedian **Jack Benny** bought a joke from comedy writer **Ace Goodman**, he sent Ace a fifty-dollar check with a note: "Your joke got lots of laughs. If you have any more, send them along."

Goodman wrote back: "Your check got lots of laughs. If you have any more, send them along."

When **W. S. Gilbert** became a big success as the lyrical half of the operetta team of Gilbert and Sullivan, he refused to grant a newspaper reporter an interview unless he was paid for the honor.

The reporter declined to pay, explaining to Gilbert that she would simply wait for the opportunity to write his obituary for free.

 Broadway producer **Billy Rose** considered himself incredibly fortunate when famed composer **Igor Stravinsky** agreed to write a ballad for one of Rose's shows.

But when Rose received the composition, he wasn't satisfied. Thinking the celebrated composer's song wasn't quite good enough, Rose sent a telegram to Stravinsky: "Your music great success. Could be sensational if you would authorize **Robert Russell Bennett** to retouch orchestration. Bennett orchestrates even the works of **Cole Porter**."

Stravinsky wired back a simple, frustrating reply: "Satisfied with great success."

 Orson Welles was hailed as the genius of Hollywood when he made the daring film *Citizen Kane*. Later, when he encountered a series of failures on the screen and in the theater, the same people who once adored him turned on him.

"When you're down and out, something always turns up," Welles said. "Usually the noses of your friends."

Most stars from Hollywood's golden years spoke in glowing terms when asked how they liked working with and romancing other stars. Thankfully, not always.

An actor who had just finished making a film with **Ginger Rogers** commented to **Cary Grant** that she wasn't very easy to know. Grant dryly observed, "Not if you're lucky, old man."

 When **Shirley Temple** was a child movie star, she was the most adored kid in America. Years later, she explained how a star can be too admired for her own good.

"I stopped believing in Santa Claus at an early age," she said. "Mother took me to see him in a department store, and he asked me for my autograph."

 The English actor **Herbert Beerbohm Tree** was engaged to star in a New York production of *Henry VIII*. When he arrived in Manhattan, he was less than impressed with his American supporting cast.

After watching the bit players who were to portray the queen's ladies-in-waiting, Tree implored them, "Ladies, just a little more virginity, if you don't mind."

 Poet **Carl Sandburg** was accused by an unhappy playwright of dozing through the performance of his play instead of evaluating his work and offering advice. "Young man," the poet explained, "sleep is an opinion."

Playwright **Oscar Wilde** was frequently attacked by critics, but not often successfully. When one of his plays was loudly panned by critics and ignored by theatergoers, Wilde defended it, saying, "The play was a great success, but the audience was a failure."

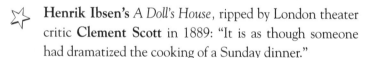

THE UNKINDEST CUTS OF ALL

Critics live in a world of their own, independent of the worth of the movies, plays, and books they exalt or demean. Or as **Will Rogers** pointed out, the only qualification a critic needs is "two seats on the aisle."

Here are critics who delight in tearing apart some of the world's great plays:

- **Henrik Ibsen's** *A Doll's House,* ripped by London theater critic **Clement Scott** in 1889: "It is as though someone had dramatized the cooking of a Sunday dinner."

- Ibsen's *Ghosts* fared worst when it opened in London in 1891, as the *Daily Telegraph* moaned: "The play performed last night is simple enough in plan and purpose, but simple only in the sense of an open drain; of a loathsome sore unbandaged; of a dirty act done publicly."

- But Ibsen got off lightly compared to the literary hisses reserved for **Shakespeare**.

Romeo and Juliet was slammed by **Samuel Pepys** in 1662 as "the worst that ever I heard in my life."

Pepys revised his opinion when he saw *A Midsummer Night's Dream*, calling it "the most insipid, ridiculous play that ever I saw in my life."

Good thing Pepys wasn't forced to sit through *Measure for Measure*, which London theater critic **James Agate** took on in the Sunday *Times* in 1933: "The most absolute bosh that ever fell from human lips."

Look Back in Anger by **John Osborne** inspired London theater critic **Milton Shulman** to write in 1956: "The play grated on me like the sustained whine of an ancient tramcar coming down a steep hill."

When the hit musical *Godspell* was revised in London, the *Guardian* recommended: "For those who missed it the first time, this is your golden opportunity—you can miss it again."

No matter what your opinion of *The World of Suzie Wong*, the musical never sank to the level of London critic **Bernard Levin**, whose search for a funny put-down (presumably while all *Daily Express* editors were on vacation) left him with this: "If you want more of China than wide sleeves and more of a play than romantic twaddle, to pay it a visit would be to enter the world of choosy wrong."

Suzie Wong . . . choosy wrong? The mind reels.

Anton Chekhov is considered one of the great writers for the theater, but not by critic Robert Garland, who wrote in the *Journal American* in 1946: "If you were to ask me what *Uncle Vanya* is about, I would say about as much as I can take."

Abie's Irish Rose was a huge Broadway hit, but not with *New Yorker* critic **Robert Benchley**, who wrote: "People laugh at this every night, which explains why democracy can never be a success."

Let's step off the stage for a moment and into the world of books, where **Jane Austen** was a literary great who utterly failed to impress another literary great, **Ralph Waldo Emerson**.

"I am at a loss to understand why people hold Miss Austen's novels at so high a rate," Emerson wrote, "which seem to me vulgar in tone, sterile in artistic invention, imprisoned in the wretched conventions of English society, without genius, wit, or knowledge of the world. Never was life so pinched and narrow."

When **Henry Fielding's** popular novel *Tom Jones* was turned into a play, theater critic **Kyle Crichton** came up with this cryptic needle: "Good Fielding. No hit."

Actors take their chances when they star in *Hamlet*. Here's the caustic **W. S. Gilbert** (of Gilbert and Sullivan fame) slaughtering **Herbert Beerbohm Tree's** star turn as the moody prince: "Do you know how they are going to decide the Shakespeare-Bacon dispute. They are going to dig up Shakespeare and dig up Bacon. They are going to set their coffins side by side, and they are going to get Tree to recite *Hamlet* to them. And the one who turns in his coffin will be the author of the play."

Now for some one-liners from critics whose witty reviews have lasted longer than the witless plays and books they slam:

Heywood Broun: "The play opened at 8:40 sharp and closed at 10:40 dull."

George S. Kaufman: "There was laughter in the back of the theater, leading to the belief that somebody was telling jokes back there."

Alexander Woollcott: "It was a tremendous success except for the minor detail that people wouldn't come to see it."

Three cuts from the dangerous **Dorothy Parker:**

1. "This must be a gift book. That is to say, a book which you wouldn't take on any other terms."

2. "This is not a novel to be tossed aside lightly. It should be thrown with great force."

3. "He's a writer for the ages—for the ages of four to eight."

FROM THE JOKE FILE

1. Two Hollywood agents are talking business. "I'm tired of these spoiled actors complaining about how we rip them off," one says.

   "Me too," the second agent agrees. "Don't we give them 90 percent of our money?"

2. Two out-of-work TV actors meet in a bar. "How's it going for you?" the first asks.

   "Couldn't be better," the second actor says. "Did you see *West Wing* last week?"

   "Yes."

   "So did I. Great show, wasn't it?"

3. The playwright and the director were shocked on opening night when the entire audience got up from their seats at the end of Act I and left the theater. The two men ran after the audience into the street. "Where are you all going?" the director shouted.

   "We'll be back next Friday," one playgoer said.

   "Why?"

   He showed them a program and pointed to the note: "Act II—one week later."

WHAT THE PROS SAY

 Radio comic **Fred Allen:** "Hollywood is a place where people from Iowa mistake each other for a star."

Newspaper columnist *Franklin Pierce Adams:* "Speaking of screen stars, there's the mosquito."

 Comic **Bob Hope:** "When she started to play, Steinway came down personally and rubbed his name off the piano."

 Comic **Greg Ray:** "You go to the ballet and see girls dancing on their tiptoes. Why don't they just get taller girls?"

 Comic **Chris Rock** (about **Bill Cosby**): "He's the only comedian I ever talked to that I felt like I was talking to a grown man, you know what I mean?"

 Radio comic **Fred Allen:** "An associate producer is the only guy in Hollywood who will associate with a producer."

 Comic **Martin Mull:** "Show business is just like high school, except you get paid."

 Radio comic **Fred Allen:** "Imitation is the sincerest form of television."

 Comic **Steve Martin:** "I handed in a script last year, and the studio didn't change one word. The word they didn't change was on page eighty-seven."

 Writer **George Bernard Shaw:** "Nothing soothes me more after a long and maddening course of piano-forte recitals than to sit and have my teeth drilled."

Comic **Groucho Marx:** "Ever since they found out that Lassie was a boy, the public has believed the worst about Hollywood."

 Comic **Steve Martin** (at the presentation of the 2001 Academy Awards): "Hosting the Oscars is like making love to a beautiful woman. It's something I only get to do when Billy Crystal's out of town."

 Comic **Victor Borge:** "In my youth, I wanted to be a great pantomime artist. Unfortunately, I had nothing to say."

 TV comic **Johnny Carson:** "If life was fair, Elvis would be alive and all the impersonators would be dead."

 Writer **Fred Allen:** "A celebrity is a person who works hard all his life to become well known, then wears dark glasses to avoid being recognized."

 TV comic **George Jessel:** "It frightens me to think what would have happened if TV had been as influential in the time of Socrates, who was not very pretty. Or of Moses, who had a great impediment of speech. Or of Jesus, whose Hebrew had a strong Galilean accent. Or of Lincoln, whose wart and shrill voice would have made Madison Avenue get rid of him immediately. It was what Mr. Lincoln said at Gettysburg that will be remembered, not how he looked or sounded on television."

MY TURN
SCENES FROM THE CUTTING-ROOM FLOOR

From *Air Force One:*

The president of the United States hides in the baggage compartment of the hijacked airplane, talking to his political adviser back in the White House.

ADVISER: So Mr. President, after you rescue the hostages, beat up the hijackers, and fly the plane to safety, could you come back to Washington and do something about the economy?

PRESIDENT: What am I, a miracle worker? If I could do anything about the economy, I wouldn't be up here flying around in circles.

CHAPTER 6

THE MOM OR THE BICYCLE?

LIFE WITH FUNNY FAMILIES

My brother-in-law asked if he could borrow my new car. I said, "Okay, but treat it like it was yours." So he sold it.

Old joke, but families can get both old and funny too.

IT'S A FUNNY LIFE

 British writer **Robert Graves** was a precocious child. When he was only four, the boy asked his mother how much money she would leave him when she died, hoping it would be enough so he could buy a bicycle.

"Surely you'd rather have me, Robby," his mother argued.

The boy considered, then said, "But I could ride to your grave on a bicycle."

72

In the novel and movie *The Great Santini*, the character of the cruel father is modeled after author **Pat Conroy's** own father. Pat's paternal grandparents took offense at the unflattering portrait of their son and disowned the writer.

But Pat's mother loved the book. She used it as evidence in court when she divorced Pat's father.

 As soon as you think you're the top dude on the cherry picker to fame, along comes your mother to set the record straight.

Here's one proud tell-all mom of Mr. Cool: **Debbie Mathers**. No, not the Beav's mom—**Eminem's** mom. Here she explains the man behind the myth to millions of rap fans: "When they look at Eminem and think what a cool, tough guy he is, they should remember that he actually lived at home with his mom until he was twenty-six."

 When he became a star on *Saturday Night Live*, **Eddie Murphy** continued to live at home with his mother, even though he was making big money on TV.

One night his mother asked Eddie to take out the garbage. Instead, he pulled out a roll of cash and gave her one hundred dollars. And that's how Eddie Murphy's younger brother got a new household chore.

 Plato had an original approach to dealing with disgruntled students at his ancient school of philosophy.

When a young student complained that there was no practical value to studying abstract mathematics (thus inventing a complaint that would echo down through the ages to our own day), Plato handed the student a few coins "so he may feel that he has gained something from my teachings."

Then Plato expelled the student from his school.

 Movie comedian **Jerry Lewis** had the kind of family life that produces comics or madmen. When he was a kid, Jerry asked his father to take him to the zoo.

"If the zoo wants you," his father replied, "let them come and get you."

 Maria Taft grew up in an accomplished family but put her legacy in perspective when she wrote a family history for a grade school class assignment:

"My great-grandfather was president of the United States. My grandfather was a senator from Ohio. My father is ambassador to Ireland. I am a Brownie."

 When **John Wesley**, who founded the Methodist Church, was a boy, his father was highly critical of his inattentive son. But his mother was more patient with the boy.

"How can you tell that blockhead the same thing twenty times over?" his father demanded.

"If I had told him but nineteen times," his mother explained, "I had wasted my breath."

In the category of what are you going to do about kids these days, consider these words of wisdom from one of our great educators:

"Children today love luxury too much. They have execrable manners, flout authority, have no respect for their elders. They no longer rise when their parents or teachers enter the room. What kind of awful creatures will they be when they grow up?"

Who bemoaned the decline of the younger generation? That would be **Socrates** in 399 B.C.

 Kids need heroes, but do heroes need kids? It's not just the demands that adulation place upon your personal life. Consider the foresight of basketball star **Charles Barkley**, who said, "Kids are great. That's one of the best things about our business, all the kids you get to meet. It's a shame they have to grow up to be regular people and come to the games and call you names."

 For another view on the subject, consider this comment from baseball star **Chili Davis**: "Growing old is mandatory; growing up is optional."

 Showing how the true capitalist spirit can be infused into an American Christmas, millionaire magazine publisher **Malcolm Forbes** once decorated his tree with five-dollar bills folded into festive holiday shapes.

FROM THE JOKE FILE

1. A three-year-old proudly put his shoes on by himself for the first time. But his mother saw the left shoe was on the right foot and said, "Your shoes are on the wrong feet, Billy."

   The boy stared at his shoes, then shook his head and said, "Don't kid me, Mom. I know they're my feet."

2. TEACHER (to student acting out): "Are you the teacher here?"
   KID: "No, I'm not."
   TEACHER: "Then stop acting like an idiot."

3. "If you worked harder in school," the father pointed out, "you wouldn't always be at the bottom of the class."

   His son shrugged. "Doesn't matter, Dad," he said. "They teach the same stuff at both ends."

4. A mother heard her three-year-old son crying. She ran into the living room and found the boy furious with his baby sister, who had a firm grip on his hair and was yanking with all her might.

   After freeing her son, the mother explained, "Don't get mad at her. She's just a baby. She doesn't understand that it hurts you."

   The boy nodded, and the mother went back into the kitchen. But not for long. She heard another cry and ran back into the living room. This time, it was the baby who was bawling. "What's wrong with her?" she asked the boy.

   "Nothing," he said. "Only now she understands."

5. Her mother thought little Amber was showing off when she told people at her new school that she was Senator Williams's daughter instead of using her own name. She told the girl just to answer simply that she was Amber Williams.

    Later the mother heard a teacher ask the girl if Senator Williams was her father. "I thought he was," Amber said. "But Mother says not."

6. The problem with kids is that they never finish what they start—like phone calls.

WHAT THE PROS SAY

Nineteenth-century lecturer **Josh Billings:** "When I was a boy of fourteen, my father was so ignorant I could hardly stand to have the old man around. But when I got to be twenty-one, I was astonished at how much the old man had learned in seven years."

Comic **Bill Cosby:** "Human beings are the only creatures on earth that allow their children to come back home."

Comic **Bob Newhart:** "My son graduated from the Catholic University of America with a degree in English literature, specializing in the poetry of Yeats. As you all know, when you pick up the classified pages you just see page after page for jobs for Yeats scholars."

TV comic *Gracie Allen:* "When I was born I was so surprised, I didn't talk for a year and a half."

Comic *Bill Cosby:* "Always end the name of your child with a vowel, so that when you yell the name will carry."

Comic *Joey Adams:* "Smack your child every day. If you don't know why—he does."

Writer *P. J. O'Rourke:* "Explain the concept of death very carefully to your child. This will make threatening him with it much more effective."

Magazine columnist *Robert Benchley:* "Dachshunds are ideal dogs for small children, as they are already stretched and pulled to such a length that the child cannot do much harm one way or the other."

Comic *Rodney Dangerfield:* "When I was a kid my parents moved a lot, but I always found them."

Comic *Joan Rivers:* "I hate housework. You make the beds, you wash the dishes, and six months later you have to start all over again."

Writer *Quentin Crisp:* "There is no need to do any housework at all. After the first four years the dirt doesn't get any worse."

Cartoonist *Charles Schulz:* "Decorate your home. It gives the illusion that your life is more interesting than it really is."

Writer **Mark Twain:** "When we were finishing our house, we found we had a little cash left over, on account of the plumber not knowing it."

Comic **Bob Hope:** "It's nice having a garden. Everything grows so fast. You dig a little hole, plant a seed, water it twice a day, and before you know it, up come the gophers."

Comic **Joey Adams:** "If it weren't for the fact that the TV set and the refrigerator are so far apart, some of us wouldn't get any exercise at all."

Writer **Mark Twain:** "In the first place, God made idiots. That was for practice. Then he made school boards."

Comic **Lenny Bruce:** "I won't say ours was a tough school, but we had our own coroner. We used to write essays like: 'What I'm Going to Be If I Grow Up.'"

Playwright **Jean Kerr:** "Now the thing about having a baby—and I can't be the first person to have noticed this—is that thereafter you have it."

Comic **Dick Gregory:** "I never believed in Santa Claus because I knew no white dude would come into my neighborhood after dark."

Comic **Paula Poundstone:** "Adults are always asking kids what they want to be when they grow up because they are looking for ideas."

Comic **Steven Wright:** "When I turned two I was really anxious, because I'd doubled my age in a year. I thought, if this keeps up, by the time I'm six I'll be ninety."

 Comic **Jerry Seinfeld:** "Remember those last few Halloweens, getting a little too old for it? Just kind of going through the motions. Bing bong. 'Come on, lady, let's go. Halloween, doorbells, candy, let's pick up the pace in there.'"

 Cartoonist **Doug Larson:** "Home computers are being called upon to perform many new functions, including the consumption of homework formerly eaten by the dog."

 Cartoonist **Charles Schulz:** "Big sisters are the crab grass in the lawn of life."

 Comic **Steven Wright:** "Babies don't need a vacation, but I still see them at the beach. I'll go over to them and say, 'What are you doing here? You've never worked a day in your life.'"

 Writer **Clarence Day:** "If your parents didn't have any children, there's a good chance that you won't have any."

 Writer **Dr. Seuss:** "Adults are obsolete children."

 Writer **Garrison Keillor:** "Selective ignorance, a cornerstone of child rearing. You don't put kids under surveillance; it might frighten you. Parents should sit tall in the saddle and look upon their troops with a noble and benevolent and extremely nearsighted gaze."

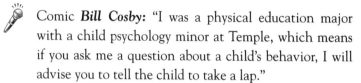 Comic **Bill Cosby:** "I was a physical education major with a child psychology minor at Temple, which means if you ask me a question about a child's behavior, I will advise you to tell the child to take a lap."

Writer **P. J. O'Rourke:** "Anything that makes your mother cry is fun."

Comic **W. C. Fields:** "Children should neither be seen nor heard from—ever again."

Comic **Rick Reynolds:** "What are kids, really, but little stupid people who live in your house and don't pay rent?"

Writer **Sam Levenson:** "The reason grandparents and grandchildren get along so well is that they have a common enemy."

Comic **Emo Philips:** "My parents threw quite a going-away party for me. According to the letter."

Comic **Drew Carey:** "I was raised by my mom. My father died when I was eight years old. At least, that's what he told us in the letter."

Comic **Jerry Seinfeld:** "Nothing in life is fun for the whole family."

MY TURN
FIVE EASY PAYMENTS

We were sitting around watching TV, and one advertiser was trying to get us to buy a complete "family" of Japanese forks. The set had forks designed for specific foods: corn forks, potato forks, steak forks—with different forks for steak medium, rare, or well done.

The guy said it would only cost us "five easy payments of $39.98."

"You ever buy anything that had complex payments?" my wife asked.

She was right. If you're willing to buy junk that already comes with its own garage-sale tags, then they're going to make it pretty easy for you to give them your money.

CHAPTER 7

THEY SPELL IT SUCCESS

BECAUSE YOU DON'T NEED TO KNOW HOW TO SPELL TO MAKE IT BIG

Success means nothing to me. But it's mutual, since I mean nothing to success.

For *New Yorker* writer **Robert Benchley**, success was neither fortune nor fame, but a way to make civilization a tolerable place in which to come in out of the rain.

"If we can develop some way in which a man can doze in public and still keep from making a monkey of himself," Benchley mused, "we have removed one of the big obstacles to human happiness in modern civilization."

That being unlikely, most of us will have to settle for fortune and fame—or at least a few laughs along the way.

IT'S A FUNNY LIFE

 A newspaper reporter asked the famous lawyer **Clarence Darrow** if hard work was responsible for his success in court.

"I guess so," Darrow answered. "I was raised on a farm. One hot day I was packing down stacks of hay, and by noon, I was totally exhausted. The next day, I left the farm, never to return, and I haven't done a day of hard work since."

 Talent can lead to success, unless you're competing in a field where talent would disqualify you. Take the advice of **David Jung**, who won the first U.S. Air Guitar Championship in 2003.

"The whole point of technique and training is to be able to give yourself to the moment and trust enough in your technique to let it go," Jung said. "Don't worry about your talent because if you had any, you wouldn't be playing air guitar."

 The rock classic "Louie Louie" was recorded by various bands in the 1950s but never became a hit. Then the **Kingsmen** recorded a version in which they slurred the vocals so you couldn't quite make out the lyrics.

A Boston radio DJ, **Woo Woo Ginsberg**, named their version the worst record of the week. He played it over and over again to prove his point.

The Kingsmen's "Louie Louie" quickly became a monster hit, selling millions of records of a song other groups couldn't give away.

A dentist who wanted to become a writer was having no luck getting his manuscripts accepted. One peeved publisher sent back his novel with this suggestion: "Why don't you go back to filling teeth? You can't write. You never could write, and you never will be able to write."

The dentist decided to give it one more try. Surprisingly, the next publisher bought the novel, and the book went on to sell a million copies.

The book? *Riders of the Purple Sage*. The dentist who couldn't write? **Zane Grey**.

A lot of success isn't about intelligence or hard work. It's about good luck. Consider **Niels Bohr**, who won the Nobel Prize for Physics in 1922, but held an unconventional attitude toward luck for a scientist.

A friend noticed that Bohr had nailed a horseshoe above the door of his cottage and questioned the physicist about whether he believed the amulet would actually bring him good luck in his work.

"Of course not," Bohr replied. "But I understand it brings you luck whether you believe or not."

The comic piano player **Victor Borge** ventured far away from his field of expertise when he bought a chicken ranch. When a friend asked if he knew anything about breeding chickens, Borge said, "No, but the chickens do."

Wilt Chamberlain was one of the greatest scorers in the history of basketball. At seven foot one, he was the dominating presence on the NBA courts for years. Despite his great success, Chamberlain was never as popular with fans as he should have been—and he knew why.

"No one," Wilt said, "roots for Goliath."

 Many literary figures and professors have amused their friends by speculating on what books they would wish to have with them if they were on a deserted island.

The British writer **G. K. Chesterton** had the winning answer in that game, saying he'd want one book only, Thomas's *Guide to Practical Shipbuilding*.

 Comic actor **Chevy Chase** knew it could be his breakthrough role if he got hired as a cast member of a new TV show called *Saturday Night Live*. At a meeting with the producers, Chase tried to convince them he was the loony comic they were looking for.

After the meeting, they all walked outside into a heavy rain. Chase ran up to a pothole filled with water and did one of his trademark flops into the puddle. "How could you say no to someone who was crazy enough to do that?" he asked the producers. They couldn't. That's how he got the job.

 Slugger **Reggie Jackson** was called Mr. October because he hit some of the biggest clutch homers in the history of baseball. But he never lost his perspective on the interplay of success and failure for any batter.

"When you've played this game for ten years and gone to bat seven thousand times and gotten two thousand hits, do you know what that really means?" Jackson pondered. "It means you've gone zero for five thousand."

 Scientist **George Washington Carver** developed more than one hundred practical uses for the common peanut. Why did he devote himself to this particular line of research?

When he was young, Carver prayed to God to explain the mysteries of the universe. "But God answered, 'That knowledge is reserved for Me alone,'" Carver reported. "So I said, 'God, tell me the mystery of the peanut.' Then God said, 'Well, George, that's more nearly your size.' And He told me."

 Tennis great **Martina Navratilova** won enough tournaments to become an expert on the subject of success. Martina's view? "Whoever said it's not whether you win or lose that counts, probably lost."

 Before **William Faulkner** became one of America's most famous writers, he struggled to find a publisher for his first novel, *Soldier's Pay*.

While working in obscurity in New Orleans, Faulkner met the already successful writer **Sherwood Anderson** and asked him to read his first effort.

Instead, Anderson struck a unique bargain with the fledgling author. "If you let me off reading your manuscript," Anderson said, "I'll get my publisher to accept it."

Faulkner knew a good deal when he heard one, and that was how his career got jump-started in 1936.

 No professional sports team has won as many titles as the New York Yankees. But when **Casey Stengel** managed the team, he understood the pressure to succeed. "The Yankees don't pay me to win every day," Casey said, "just two out of three."

 Composer **Wolfgang Mozart** was trying to help a music student who asked the master how to write a symphony. Mozart suggested that at such a young age, the student should concentrate on writing shorter compositions first.

"But you composed symphonies when you were only ten," the student argued.

"True," Mozart said, "but I didn't have to ask how."

BONUS LAUGH
THERE ARE MORE PEOPLE WHO WILL TELL YOU HOW TO SUCCEED THAN THERE ARE SUCCESS STORIES

Here's some unusual advice from six people who actually got where they were going (at least until they made a wrong turn at Russia).

1. **David Sarnoff,** TV pioneer: "A kick in the pants sends you further along than a friendly handshake."

2. Violinist **Niccolò Paganini:** "Toil, solitude, prayer."

3. Car manufacturer **Henry Ford:** "When you start a thing, finish it."

4. **James Burrill Angell,** president of the University of Michigan: "Grow antennae, not horns."

5. Industrialist **Andrew Carnegie:** "Do your duty and a little more, and the future will take care of itself."

6. French emperor **Napoleon:** "I have known the limitations of my legs. I have known the limitations of my eyes. I have never been able to know the limitations of my working capacity."

FROM THE JOKE FILE

1. The company president went into the board chairman's office to find out how he'd done at a corporate seminar on memory improvement.

   "A high-powered experience," the chairman said. "They taught me techniques that improved my memory 32 percent."

   "Sounds like a big success," the president said. "What was the seminar called?"

   The chairman thought for a moment, then snapped his fingers. "What do you call that red flower with the thorns and the long stem?" he asked the president.

   "You mean a rose?"

"Yes, that's it," the chairman said. He buzzed his intercom to get his secretary. "Rose," he said, "what was the name of that seminar?"

2. If at first you don't succeed, you're running about par for the course.

3. If at first you don't succeed, don't try skydiving.

WHAT THE PROS SAY

 Comic actor **W. C. Fields:** "If at first you don't succeed, try, try again. Then quit. There's no point in being a damn fool about it."

 Writer **Quentin Crisp:** "If at first you don't succeed, failure may be your style."

 Comic **Lily Tomlin:** "Sometimes I worry about being a success in a mediocre world."

 Newspaper columnist **Earl Wilson:** "Success is simply a matter of luck. Ask any failure."

 Comic **Jonathan Winters:** "I couldn't wait for success, so I went ahead without it."

Comic **Steven Wright:** "When everything is coming your way, you're in the wrong lane."

 Magazine columnist **Robert Benchley:** "It took me fifteen years to discover I had no talent for writing. But I couldn't give it up because by that time I was too famous."

 Writer **François Voltaire:** "Behind every successful man stands a surprised mother-in-law."

 Writer **Quentin Crisp:** "Never keep up with the Joneses. Drag them down to your level."

 Comic **Dick Gregory:** "You know why Madison Avenue advertising has never done well in Harlem? We're the only ones who know what it means to be Brand X."

 Writer **James Thurber:** "Early to rise and early to bed makes a male healthy, wealthy, and dead."

 Comic **Steven Wright:** "You can't have everything. Where would you put it?"

 Nineteenth-century lecturer **Josh Billings:** "If a man should happen to reach perfection in this world, he would have to die immediately to enjoy himself."

 TV comic **John Belushi:** "I owe it all to little chocolate doughnuts."

MY TURN
FROM THE TO-DO LISTS OF FAMOUS PEOPLE: POP SINGER CHRISTINA AGUILERA

1. Meet with belly consultant: new trends—twist left or right?

2. Meet with butt consultant: Are we falling behind the curve?

3. Meet with bust consultant: results of the latest poll— how much does the public want?

4. Meet with time-and-fame consultant: thirteenth or fourteenth minute—anyone know?

CHAPTER 8

ANYWHERE BUT PHILADELPHIA

ON THE ROAD TO COMEDY

"Boy, those French," comic **Steve Martin** marveled, "they have a different word for everything!"

Travel is broadening and not just if you eat too much French food. I once took a magazine assignment to travel across the American West searching for the best country-fried steak. Didn't find it either, but there are some jobs you don't mind failing at.

As we hit the open road, remember that if we find something funny, we'll just back up and roll over it a few times.

IT'S A FUNNY LIFE ON THE ROAD

 Traveling by train may bring you into contact with a different class of people—the upper class. It happened to British symphony conductor **Thomas Beecham**, who was riding in a nonsmoking car when a rich snob lit a cigarette, then said, "I'm sure you won't mind if I smoke."

"No, ma'am," Beecham replied, "if you don't mind that I get sick."

As a wealthy matron, the woman was not accustomed to being rebuffed. "I don't think you know who I am," she said. "I am one of the directors' wives."

"Madam," Beecham said, "if you were the director's only wife, I'd still get sick."

 In 1903 the San Francisco doctor **Horatio Jackson** and mechanic **Sewall Crocker** set off in a twenty-horsepower Winton in a daring attempt to become the first people to cross the entire country in a car.

At that time, there were no paved roads between towns and fewer than two hundred miles of paved roads in the cities. One more problem: no gas stations.

Getting lost one day while on their long, slow journey, Jackson and Crocker stopped and asked a woman for directions to the next town. She pointed up a dirt road, and they drove off.

An hour later, the road ended at a farm. The farmwife told the drivers they'd have to go all the way back the way they'd come.

As they drove back, they passed the woman who had given them the wrong directions to begin with. She had a good explanation for why she'd done it: Her mother (the farmwife) had never seen a car before, and this would probably be the only chance she'd ever have.

Baseball great **Satchel Paige** was a sportswriter's dream, coming up with some of the most original quotes ever heard in a dugout, including this gem: "Airplanes may kill you, but they ain't likely to hurt you."

In the 1930s, tough-talking head of the FBI **J. Edgar Hoover** took a road trip across the United States. This is what he found: "Dens of vice and corruption, haunted by nomadic prostitutes, hardened criminals, white slavers, and promiscuous college students."

What was Hoover referring to? Trailer parks.

 When United Airlines started commercial flights, the first airline stewardesses were also nurses who had to take care of passengers when they grew airsick, which was often.

But that's not all the stewardesses were expected to do. Before passengers got on board, the stewardesses joined the rest of the crew in pulling the plane from the hangar onto the runway.

 Baseball slugger **Richie Allen**: "I'll play first, third, left. I'll play anywhere—except Philadelphia."

New York. Los Angeles. America's two great metropolises—one vertical, the other horizontal—in a never-ending rivalry. But which city is a magnet of culture and round-the-clock excitement, and which is the cesspool of stupidity?

Tough call—and it takes someone who has lived in both cities to make that call. Someone like poet **Randall Jarrell**, who was bi-metropolitan.

"How can people who live in New York make remarks about southern California?" he asked. "They ought to be put in asylums, which would at least be a change from New York City."

 In the movie *The Razor's Edge*, **Clifton Webb** made the point often muttered by residents of both coasts: "I've never been able to understand why, when there's so much space in the world, people should deliberately choose to live in the Middle West."

 Writer **George Jean Nathan** described Hollywood as "Ten million dollars' worth of intricate and highly ingenious machinery functioning elaborately to put skin on baloney."

 Writer **Norman Mailer** spent the winters working on his books at his second home in Cape Cod, Massachusetts. Why did he like to do his writing up there instead of Manhattan?

"You don't feel sorry for yourself that you're missing anything," Mailer explained, "because nothing is happening."

FROM THE JOKE FILE

1. An American in Paris couldn't get a taxi driver to understand that he wanted to return to his hotel. One spoke no French, the other no English.

    Then the visitor got a bright idea. He showed the driver a pack of matches with the hotel's name on the cover. Twenty minutes later, the taxi pulled up in front of the match factory.

2. Why does California have golden hills, Hawaii white sandy beaches, and New Jersey toxic waste dumps?

    Jersey had first choice.

3. Two Boston matrons were touring Los Angeles when one complained of the stifling heat. "What can you expect?" her companion said in commiseration. "We're three thousand miles from the ocean."

4. A traveler from Arkansas visited a church one Sunday while on a trip to Ohio. During the sermon, the preacher called to the congregation, "Stand up, brothers and sisters, if you want to go to heaven." Everyone in the church stood up—except for the visitor.

    "Friend," the preacher said, "are you telling us you wish to go down instead of up?"

    "Actually, I was thinking of going back to Arkansas," the traveler said. "But if I can't do that, heaven wouldn't be too bad as a second choice."

5. Three men were hunting deer deep in the mountains of Montana. The first two dressed in camouflage outfits, scouted the terrain, took up positions in the woods, spent the entire day there, and never saw a single deer.

   The third man, who had never gone hunting before, put on a three-piece business suit, opened a copy of the *New York Times,* and sat down in a comfortable chair at the edge of camp. At the end of the day, when the other two hunters returned, they were stunned to see that he'd shot three deer.

   "You don't know the first thing about hunting," one of the veterans said. "How'd you manage to shoot three of them?"

   The rookie shrugged and said, "When the deer saw me dressed like a New Yorker, they figured I couldn't shoot and was probably drunk, so they came right into camp."

WHAT THE PROS SAY

 Comic *George Carlin:* "What does it mean to preboard? Do you get on before you get on?"

 Comic *Jerry Seinfeld:* "I like staying in hotels. I enjoy hotels. I like tiny soap. I pretend that it's normal soap and my muscles are huge."

 Comic *Shelley Berman:* "A hotel is a place where the minute your shower temperature is adjusted, somebody signals the guy next door to flush his toilet."

Comic **Groucho Marx:** "Room service? Send up a larger room."

 TV comic **George Gobel:** "The National Safety Council estimated that 354 people would be killed in traffic accidents over the holiday weekend. So far only 172 have been killed. Some of you folks aren't trying."

 Comic **Joan Rivers:** "The last airline I flew was bad. They didn't need to show a movie. Every ten seconds your life passed before your eyes."

 Comic **Jerry Seinfeld:** "Are there keys to a plane? Maybe that's what those delays are . . . They tell you it's something mechanical because they don't want to come on the P.A. system: 'Ladies and gentlemen, we're going to be delayed here on the ground for a while . . . This is so embarrassing . . . I left the keys to the plane in my apartment. They're in this big ashtray by the front door. I'm sorry, I'll run back and get them.'"

 Cartoonist **Doug Larson:** "If all the cars in the United States were placed end to end, it would probably be Labor Day weekend."

 Magazine columnist **Robert Benchley:** "In America there are two classes of travel: first class and with children."

 TV comic **David Letterman:** "Fall is my favorite season in Los Angeles, watching the birds change color and fall from the trees."

Comic **Mort Sahl:** "Beverly Hills is very exclusive. Even the fire department won't make house calls."

 Newspaper columnist **Herb Caen:** "If all the world's a stage, then San Francisco is the cast party."

 Comic **Drew Carey:** "Vegas is everything that's *right* with America. You can do whatever you want, twenty-four hours a day. They've effectively legalized everything there. You don't *have* to gamble if you don't want to."

 Radio comic **Fred Allen:** "I have just returned from Boston. It is the only thing to do if you find yourself up there."

 Playwright **George S. Kaufman:** "I went through Boston once, but it was closed."

 Writer **Raymond Chandler:** "I guess God made Boston on a wet Sunday."

 Movie comic **Groucho Marx:** "It isn't necessary to have relatives in Kansas City in order to be unhappy."

 Comic **Dudley Moore:** "People down South are incredibly polite. Even their war was civil."

 Comic **Minnie Pearl:** "He said, 'I bet she don't know a goose from a gander.' I said, 'Well, at Grinder's Switch, we don't worry about that. We just put them all out there together and let 'em figure it out for themselves.'"

 Comic **Lenny Bruce:** "I hate small towns because once you've seen the cannon in the park there's nothing else to do."

Writer **Alexander Woollcott:** "A small town is one where there is no place to go where you shouldn't."

 Radio comic **Fred Allen:** "The first thing that strikes a visitor to Paris is a taxi."

 Comic **Billy Connolly:** "The great thing about Glasgow is that if there's a nuclear attack it'll look exactly the same afterwards."

 English writer **Alan Coren:** "[The French] believe themselves to be great lovers—an easy trap to fall into when you're permanently drunk."

 Russian comic **Yakov Smirnoff:** "In Russia we only had two TV channels. Channel One was propaganda. Channel Two consisted of a KGB officer telling you, 'Turn back at once to Channel One.'"

 Writer **Will Rogers:** "Rome has more churches and less preaching in them than any city. Everybody wants to see where Saint Peter was buried, but nobody wants to try to live like him."

 Writer **George Bernard Shaw:** "I showed my appreciation of my native land in the usual Irish way by getting out of it as soon as I possibly could."

 Writer **Ring Lardner:** "There's an old saw to the effect that the sun never sets on the British Empire. While we were there, it never even rose."

MY TURN
FLYING SOLO

Have you ever been the only passenger on an airplane? I don't mean when your flying buddy wants to shake up your life on his tiny stomach-churner. I mean the only passenger on a commercial airline flight.

Happened to me on an early-morning flight from L.A. to San Luis Obispo, an hour up the coast. Two pilots, two flight attendants, and me.

I thought, At last, I can have any seat on the plane I want. Not so. I was told I had to sit in row seven so I would balance out the plane. With the two pilots and one attendant sitting in front, the other attendant and I were responsible for making sure the plane didn't tip up on its nose.

When you're one passenger in a cattle herd, you can ignore the attendant's warning routine about how if the plane's going to crash they'd like to keep you busy for the final forty-five seconds so you don't pester them with your upcoming separation into fifty-six indistinct parts.

You can't ignore the flight attendant's spiel when you're the only passenger on the plane because the attendant walks up and stands in your face as she explains final procedures to you.

"The plane has four emergency exits," she told me.

"Best-case scenario," I replied, "I can only use one."

CHAPTER 9

MILK'S LEAP TOWARD IMMORTALITY

AND OTHER FUNNY FOODS FOR THOUGHT

Yogi Berra may have been the funniest guy to play the game of baseball. But he could also be pretty amusing at the dinner table.

After ordering a pizza at one of his favorite restaurants, Yogi had second thoughts. "You better cut the pizza in four pieces," he told the cook, "because I'm not hungry enough to eat six."

While you're waiting for your own four-piece pizza, let's see what's cooking in the comedy kitchen.

IT'S A FUNNY LIFE

 German opera singer **Ernestine Schumann-Heink** loved good food as much as she loved to sing. One night she sat down to a big meal in a fancy restaurant when fellow opera singer and trencherman **Enrico Caruso** came into the dining room.

Caruso saw Schumann-Heink digging into a huge steak and asked, "Surely you are not going to eat that alone?"

"No, no, not alone," she assured him, "with potatoes."

 One Thanksgiving **Calvin Coolidge** and his wife entertained friends in their Massachusetts home. At dinner, the maid came in to present the large turkey before it was carved. The president's guests were mistreated to one of those classic dinner party nightmares when the maid tripped and the turkey skidded across the floor.

The quick-thinking Mrs. Coolidge rescued the situation. She helped the maid to her feet and said, "Now take this turkey back into the kitchen and bring out the *other* one."

 Movie director **Alfred Hitchcock** was a man of large appetites. So he was frustrated one night when invited to a friend's house for dinner, only to be served a meal too genteel and too scant in portion.

As Hitchcock was departing, his hostess said politely, "I do hope you will dine with us again soon."

"By all means," Hitchcock said. "Let's start now."

 British politician **Austen Chamberlain** was the guest of honor at a London dinner party in 1921. As Chamberlain launched into a long discourse on the political situation in England and Ireland, the hostess noticed that her butler was tipsy.

Hoping to avoid a scene in front of her guests, she called the butler over and gave him a note: "You are drunk. Leave the room at once."

Instead of leaving to sober up downstairs, the butler nodded gravely. He put the note on a tray, walked around the table, and handed it to Austen Chamberlain.

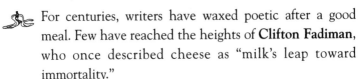 For centuries, writers have waxed poetic after a good meal. Few have reached the heights of **Clifton Fadiman**, who once described cheese as "milk's leap toward immortality."

Unlike other new fathers, **Jared Lorenzen**, a 295-pound quarterback for the University of Kentucky, didn't mind getting up to help his wife feed the new baby.

"Getting up in the middle of the night for feedings at one, three, and five," he said, "kind of like I do for myself."

Broadcaster **Curt Gowdy** went out for a beer with Yankee manager **Casey Stengel** after a game in Cleveland. Casey chugged his beer in a single gulp. Gowdy asked him why he drank so fast.

"I drink it like that ever since the accident," Stengel said.

"You were in an accident?" Gowdy asked.

"Yeah," Casey explained, "somebody knocked over my beer."

In the category of It Must Have Seemed Like a Good Idea at the Time, a couple of South African businessmen opened a restaurant called Nelson's Chicken and Gravy Land.

Nelson Mandela didn't think it was such a great idea. As president of South Africa, he was too busy leading his nation into a new era of freedom to lend his name to dishes like Nelson's Freedom Meal.

The restaurant owners were surprised when Mandela threatened to take them to court if they didn't stop using his name to sell chicken. After all, isn't that what freedom is all about?

FROM THE JOKE FILE

1. A woman sent her not-too-bright husband to the supermarket to pick up some supplies. When he didn't return an hour later, she went looking for him, worried something had gone wrong.

   She found him in the frozen-food aisle staring at the frozen orange juice because the label said, "Concentrate."

2. Two construction workers went into a restaurant at lunchtime, ordered coffee, then pulled their own sandwiches out of bags and began to eat. The manager came over to their table and said, "You can't eat your own sandwiches in here."

   So the men shrugged and swapped sandwiches.

3. Americans are getting stronger. Fifty years ago, you needed a pickup truck to hold ten dollars' worth of groceries. Twenty years ago, it took two people to carry home ten dollars' worth of food from the store. Now any five-year-old can do it.

4. It was a long flight on an economy airline, so the businessman was happy when the flight attendant asked if he would like dinner.

    "Great," he said, "what are my choices?"

    "Yes or no," she replied.

WHAT THE PROS SAY

 Comic **Jerry Seinfeld:** "There are so many subtle insults in a lot of these products. What the hell is Chicken-of-the-Sea tuna? There's no chickens in the sea. What do they think, they're afraid to tell us it's a fish? Afraid we won't understand?"

 Comic **Gracie Allen:** "This recipe is certainly silly. It says to separate two eggs, but it doesn't say how far to separate them."

 Radio comic **Fred Allen:** "He dreamed he was eating shredded wheat and woke up to find the mattress half gone."

Comic **Phyllis Diller:** "If your husband wants to lick the beaters on the mixer, shut them off before you give them to him."

 Comic **George Carlin:** "The other night I ate at a real nice family restaurant. Every table had an argument going."

 Comic **Buddy Hackett:** "As a child my family's menu consisted of two choices: Take it or leave it."

 Writer **Helen Gurley Brown:** "I know one fortunate little boy whose parents told him the facts of life so satisfactorily, he said in the next breath, 'Now tell me how they make peanut butter.'"

 Nineteenth-century lecturer **Josh Billings:** "If it wasn't for faith, there would be no living in this world; we couldn't even eat hash with any safety."

 Writer **Fran Lebowitz:** "Thin, almost transparent slices of lemon do indeed go a long way in dressing up a meal, but they should not be counted as a separate vegetable."

 Comic **Rita Rudner:** "I was a vegetarian until I started leaning toward the sunlight."

 Writer **A. Whitney Brown:** "I became a vegetarian not so much because I love animals but because I hate plants."

 Comic **Steven Wright:** "I was at this restaurant. The sign said: BREAKFAST ANYTIME. So I ordered French toast in the Renaissance."

Writer **William Burroughs:** "You can't fake quality any more than you can fake a good meal."

 Writer **Margaret Halsey:** "We hurried in, and an absentminded waitress gave us a pot of tea, supplemented after fifteen minutes by a piece of steak which had evidently been put to bed for the night and resented being disturbed."

 Comic **Gracie Allen:** "He said, 'Let's have a drink. Bottoms up.' And I said, 'Isn't that an awkward position?'"

 Writer **Fran Lebowitz:** "People have been cooking and eating for thousands of years, so if you are the very first to have thought of adding fresh lime juice to scalloped potatoes try to understand that there must be a reason for this."

 Writer **Robert Orben:** "The next time you feel like complaining, remember that your garbage disposal probably eats better than 30 percent of the people in the world."

MY TURN
FOODS OF THE STARS

I'm opening a new movie-theme restaurant, an all-you-can-eat buffet called *Gladiator* because if you've got a hungry guy in your family, he'll be "glad he ate here."

Here's what I've got on the movie menu so far:

A Fishstick Called Wanda: Seafood with personality, served with Some Like It Hot Sauce, spiced up with a touch of Jack Lemmon.

The Big Chili: In the only bowl big enough to feed all your nostalgic friends.

M*A*S*H *Potatoes:* Now you can enjoy those authentic "mess hall spuds," just like the potatoes that made the Korean War such a popular dining spot.

The Peanut Butter and Grape Jelly of Wrath Sandwich: Made from the angriest fruit in California.

Stout of Africa: The only beer brewed by tormented Danish farmers. Three chugs and you'll be mumbling, "I'm about to buy the farm in Africa."

Animal House Crackers: The cookie of choice for food fights.

Citizen Candy Kane: Handmade exclusively for the exclusive by our little candy maker, Rose Budd.

CHAPTER 10

CASEY AT THE BAR

JOKES FOR JOCKS

When the New York Mets were hopeless and **Casey Stengel** their manager, **Rod Kanehl** was the skipper's favorite hustling utility player. In one game, Hot Rod was sent out to pinch-run, then hustled in to score from second on a wild pitch.

Casey liked Kanehl's effort so much, he told him to stay in the game.

"Where should I play?" Hot Rod asked.

"I don't care," Casey said. "Play any place you want."

Kanehl stayed in at short. Wouldn't you?

That's why sports are so much fun: We either care way too much or not at all. If you're really good, you can play any place you want. And if you're really bad, somewhere out there is a team that will let you play any place you want just for laughs.

IT'S A FUNNY LIFE
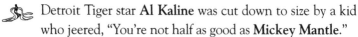

In baseball **Joe Garagiola** made a name for himself only when he stopped being a catcher and became a broadcaster. Or as Yankee manager **Casey Stengel** put it, "Joe, when they list all the great catchers, you'll be there—listening."

Detroit Tiger star **Al Kaline** was cut down to size by a kid who jeered, "You're not half as good as **Mickey Mantle**."

Kaline took it in stride, pointing out, "Son, nobody is half as good as Mickey Mantle."

When **Hack Wilson** was a slugger, plenty of baseball players drank to excess, Hack included. His manager on the Brooklyn Dodgers, **Max Carey**, tried to sober him up by showing Hack what happened when he dropped a worm in a glass of gin: the worm died.

Hack laughed off the lesson—then kept drinking. "Skipper," he said, "it just proves if you drink gin you'll never have worms."

Tris Speaker was one of the greatest center fielders of all time and a hellion as a young player. He was described by one newspaper writer as "a little wild, but he wasn't a loafer. I guess he couldn't hold still long enough to loaf properly."

The golfer **Tommy Bolt** had a great swing and a bad temper. During one tournament, he kept making difficult putts, only to have the ball spin off the lip on cup after cup.

Finally, Bolt could stand no more. He threw down his putter and shouted at the heavens, "Why don't you come down and fight like a man?"

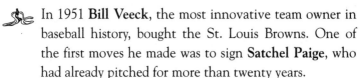

In 1951 **Bill Veeck**, the most innovative team owner in baseball history, bought the St. Louis Browns. One of the first moves he made was to sign **Satchel Paige**, who had already pitched for more than twenty years.

Everyone else thought Paige was way, way over the hill. But Satchel was far from done. He had a better year than most pitchers half his age.

"Everybody kept telling me he was through," Veeck reflected, "but that was understandable. They thought he was only human."

Enjoying their job is not as important for boxers as being able to take a punch and give more than you get. But if anybody seemed to enjoy himself before, during, and after a fight, it was the heavyweight champ **Muhammad Ali**.

Yet even Ali took a realistically downbeat approach to his craft. "It's just a job," he said. "Grass grows, birds fly, waves pound the sand. I beat people up."

Talent is the key to success in sports. Also confidence. Not to mention luck. And the ability to find the opponent's weakness—that's the key to success in sports. Oh yeah, one more thing: not getting bogged down in too many keys.

Basketball star **Charles Barkley** had that winning attitude nailed, as he made clear with this play-off prediction: "I think that the team that wins game five will win the series. Unless we lose game five."

 From pitching great **Roger Clemens** to tennis legend **Martina Navratilova**, we've seen great athletes who retire but just can't stay away from their sport. Do they come back for the glory? The big money? Yes and yes.

Then there's oft-retired, just-as-oft-returned heavyweight boxer **George Foreman**, who climbed back into the ring for a reason all his own. "I want to keep fighting because it is the only thing that keeps me out of the hamburger joints," Foreman explained. "If I don't fight, I'll eat this planet."

 Very few people can hit a major-league fastball. Toss in the sinker, the slider, and the knuckler, and pitching has been known to reduce strong men to careers in insurance sales.

There's something about the intensity of the struggle to stick in the majors that brings out the jerk in many big-league players. Or maybe it's the million-dollar contracts.

Then there's the rare free spirit who plays his own game, like former Yankee outfielder **Mickey Rivers**. Here are three gems that put Mickey in the same league with **Casey Stengel** and **Yogi Berra**:

1. Rivers on his relationship with **George Steinbrenner** and **Billy Martin**: "Me and George and Billy are two of a kind."

2. Rivers reevaluating Yankee teammate **Reggie Jackson's** boast that his IQ was 160: "Out of what, a thousand?"

3. Rivers explaining why baseball is a tricky game: "Pitching is 80 percent of the game, and the other half is hitting and fielding."

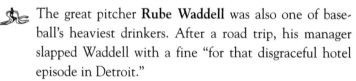 The great pitcher **Rube Waddell** was also one of baseball's heaviest drinkers. After a road trip, his manager slapped Waddell with a fine "for that disgraceful hotel episode in Detroit."

"I'm innocent," Waddell claimed, thinking he could convince the skipper to take back the fine. "There is no Hotel Episode in Detroit."

 If you buy into the TV commercials, then you might be tempted to buy incredibly expensive sports shoes under the impression that somehow they're going to improve your game.

If, however, you listen to basketball star **Charles Barkley**, they're going to have a hard time selling you overpriced anything.

"These are my new shoes," Sir Charles said. "They're good shoes. They won't make you rich like me. They won't make you rebound like me. They definitely won't make you handsome like me. They'll only make you have shoes like me. That's it."

 Will we ever settle the debate about which sport requires the most brainpower to play?

Baseball pitcher **Jim Bouton** gave it a shot, claiming, "Baseball players are smarter than football players. How often do you see a baseball team penalized for too many men on the field?"

 Leo Durocher was a die-hard baseball player, but he earned his nickname, Leo the Lip, for his dirt-kicking antics as a manager.

In one game he stormed out of the dugout to argue a call and went toe to toe with the umpire, who tossed him off the field. Durocher later admitted, "I made a game effort to argue, but two things were against me: the umpires and the rules."

 Baseball is a game of infinite strategy—and occasional simplicity. Here's pitcher **Lefty Gomez** explaining his approach to the game: "One rule I had was make your best pitch and back up third base. That relay might get away, and you've got another shot at him."

When **Wiley Peck** played basketball for Mississippi State, he took the in-your-face attitude to a new level—combining it with the ironic self-discovery we associate with English lit majors.

During a game, Peck slam-dunked a ball "in your face!" But the slam dunk bounced hard off the rim, hit Peck in his own face, and knocked him out.

 Every major-league hitter has a pitcher he'd just as well not face. But Yankee slugger **Mickey Mantle** had a special reason to avoid Dodger pitcher **Don Drysdale**.

"I hated to bat against Drysdale," the Mick said. "After he hit you, he'd come around, look at the bruise on your arm, and say, 'Do you want me to sign it?'"

 Few major-league managers like the chore of sending a player down to the minors. But Yankee manager **Casey Stengel** faced up to it in his own style.

"Son, we'd like to keep you around this season," he explained as he held the door open for a young player who wasn't cutting it. "But we're going to try and win a pennant."

Stengel, like all managers, had to deal with a team's struggle to get out of a slump. During one stretch when the Yankees couldn't get untracked, Casey moaned to reporters, "We are in such a slump that even the ones that aren't drinking aren't hitting."

When slugger **Reggie Jackson** played for the New York Yankees, he raised the level of Bronx cheers everywhere but in the Bronx. All right, sometimes in the Bronx, too.

Didn't bother Jackson a bit. As he proudly told the press, "Fans don't boo nobodies."

 Most professional athletes don't like to talk about the extraordinary salaries they command for excelling at games they once played for fun when they were kids.

Then there was the eccentric and beloved relief pitcher **Tug McGraw**, who put his good fortune in perspective when he signed a lucrative contract.

"Ninety percent I'll spend on good times, women, and Irish whiskey," Tug admitted. "The other 10 percent I'll probably waste."

 Satchel Paige was one of the greatest pitchers in baseball history, blazing a path of strikeouts through the Negro Leagues with his Hesitation Pitch and his Bat Dodger.

After the game's color barrier was finally broken, Paige made his major-league debut with the Cleveland Indians at the age of forty-one, long past the time most players are retired.

Putting his career and the nation's history in perspective, Paige said, "Baseball has turned me from a second-class citizen to a second-class immortal."

FROM THE JOKE FILE

1. As a boxing trainer, Mac was a master at using psychology to motivate his fighters. During the championship bout, Sluggo was being beaten badly.

    In between rounds, Mac screamed at him, "You're a bum. I want you to get out there and fight. Stick and move. Use your right. Throw the hook. Win this fight, or you're through, you big jerk."

    And it worked. Sluggo knocked out the champ in the next round because if there was one thing he hated, it was being yelled at.

2. An arrogant golfer tossed his club to his new caddy and said, "What do you think of my game, kid?"

    "I think it's great, sir," the caddy said, "although I still prefer golf."

3. A rookie hunter was going into the wilderness for his first solo hunt. "I hear there are some nasty grizzlies up there," he said to a veteran guide. "What kind of rifle should I carry?"

    "It doesn't matter what kind you carry," the guide told him. "What counts is how fast you carry it."

4. After slicing five drives in a row, the golfer got fed up, hurled his brand-new set of clubs into the lake, and stormed off.

    Five minutes later he came back, dove into the lake, and retrieved his clubs. Zipping open the bag, he took out his car keys and threw the clubs back into the water.

WHAT THE PROS SAY

 Newspaper columnist **Herb Caen:** "The clock doesn't matter in baseball. Time stands still or moves backwards. Theoretically, one game could go on forever. Some seem to."

 Comic **Jerry Seinfeld:** "You win the gold, you feel good. You win the bronze, you think, Well, at least I got something. But you win that silver, that's like: Congratulations, you almost won. Of all the losers, you came in first of that group. You're the number one loser."

 Newspaper writer **Jim Bishop:** "Golf is played by twenty million mature American men whose wives think they are out having fun."

 Comic **Joan Rivers:** "I don't work out. If God had wanted us to bend over, He would have put diamonds on the floor."

 Comic **Martin Mull:** "The trouble with jogging is that the ice falls out of your glass."

 Comic **Phyllis Diller:** "The reason the pro tells you to keep your head down is so you can't see him laughing."

 Sportscaster **Joe Garagiola:** "Nolan Ryan is pitching much better now that he has his curveball straightened out."

 Comic **Bob Hope:** "If you watch a game, it's fun. If you play it, it's recreation. If you work at it, it's golf."

Writer **Erma Bombeck:** "If a man watches three football games in a row, he should be declared legally dead."

 Comic **Jerry Seinfeld:** "Racehorses must get to the end and go, 'We were just here. What was the point of that? This is where we were! That was the longest possible route you could take to get where you wanted to be! Why don't we just stay here? I would've been first.'"

Comic strip writer **Johnny Hart:** "Let me get this straight. The less I hit the ball, the better I'm doing. Then why do it at all?"

 Comic **Jerry Seinfeld:** "The luge is the only sport I've ever seen that you could have people competing in it against their will. And it would be exactly the same."

MY TURN
WHEN BASEBALL WAS JUNG

Dr. "Lefty" Markowitz, Gestalt therapist and lead-off hitter for the Psychologists, singles to left, where Philosopher speedster Bernardo Flin, a Platonic noninterventionist, watches the ball roll to the fence while he considers the question: What is a single after all?

Meanwhile, Dr. Markowitz stops halfway to first to analyze his compulsive need to score.

The Philosophers' metaphysician, Sparky Zum, playing center field because of the theoretical injury to regular Reggie

Conundrum, retrieves the ball and examines the laces for cabalistic messages.

"I came to the conclusion," Dr. Markowitz writes in his journal as he rounds first, "that if I was hitting good, my batting wasn't average anymore. Suddenly, first base was clear for me."

Batting second, Dr. Bucky Pinhalter, a leading fat-free guilt-ologist, strikes out on three pitches because they remind him of his mother.

Switch-hitting third baseman Dr. Paoli Zink, Ole number 33, takes note of the enigmatic significance of the number three in his game plan. By the time he prepares an outline for a research paper on the subject, Philosopher pitcher Carl Karl, a noncommitted existentialist, sneaks two screwballs past him.

Lefty Markowitz calls time to ask the ump for an interpretation of his desire to steal second. When the ump explains that stealing is encouraged by leading baseball authorities, Dr. M asks him to look deeper.

On the next pitch, Zink makes a definite commitment and strokes an Aristotelian curveball up the gap in right.

Harvey "Crush" Wigglesworth, the fleet-footed Randian determinist, calls for the ball before it is actually hit. But Sparky Zum in center, who has converted to neo-Marxian sophistry between pitches, argues that all fly balls are the result of the team's labor. Therefore, they should field the ball together, until a popular vote can determine whether catching it is in the best interest of the fans.

When the dust settles, Dr. Zink is out at first, but feels good about himself. When Lefty gets caught in a rundown, second baseman and linguist Oral "Spud" Jones, Ph.D., refuses to tag Lefty out, arguing that "out" is not the opposite of "safe," that he could only tag the runner either "in" or "dangerous."

By the time that theory has been proposed, rebutted, and established as a school of metaphysical inquiry, Lefty is standing safely or "inly" on third.

The next batter, designated analyst Dr. Mandrake Gleeb, takes the first two pitches. "Stee-rike," offers the ump twice.

"Is the umpire afraid to confront his real feelings by hiding behind a mask?" Dr. Gleeb ponders. "Besides which, the pitch was outside by a mile, you blind obsessive-compulsive."

With two outs, more or less, Gleeb uses reverse psychology and bunts back to the pitcher. Faced with the sudden realization that the universe either is or is not perfect, Philosopher pitcher Karl sits down on the mound to reflect on the meaninglessness of the concept of "winning" in an infinite game mode.

Zen third baseman Mik Da Matejan races to the mound, where he accepts the consequences of his intervention in the grand scheme of things, after which he fires the ball toward home.

Dr. M wavers halfway down from third while he tries to assimilate the full implications of going "home," as catcher Prometheus Cube, a veteran ironist, blocks the plate, but from the back side, to make a statement about the absurdity of life and baseball, insomuch as baseball is a part of life.

As darkness nears, the runner finally accepts the paternalistic dream interpretation of the third-base coach, who resembles his father, and slides home safely under the tag.

At the end of the top of the first inning, the score stands Psychologists 1, Philosophers 0. After which the game is called on account of paradox.

CHAPTER 11

CHEAP LANDSLIDES

LAUGHING WITH THE POLITICIANS

"Politicians are wonderful people," writer **P. J. O'Rourke** said, "as long as they stay away from things they don't understand, such as working for a living."

Working is not a governmental priority because politicians already have a full-time job—running for office. Running the government is something they do in their spare time.

Amazingly, politicians also hold down a third job—providing comedy writers with plenty of material.

IT'S A FUNNY LIFE

 When **John F. Kennedy** was running for president, critics often accused his father of using his vast wealth to buy the election. After Kennedy won, the president joked that he had received a wire from his father telling him, "Don't buy one more vote than you need. I'm not going to pay for a landslide."

At least, we think he was joking.

 Sick of all the negative campaigning in our presidential elections? If it gets any worse, we're likely see ads warning us, "If he is elected, murder, robbery, rape, adultery, and incest will be openly taught and practiced."

Sound far-fetched? Not in 1800, when the campaign staff of President **John Adams** made that claim against the incumbent's rival, **Thomas Jefferson**.

For his part, Jefferson's campaign retaliated by accusing Adams of planning to give the country back to England. Why England would want it back was never explained.

Despite their slanderous campaign tactics, Jefferson and Adams were men of historic stature. They would be shocked by today's negative campaigning—shocked that it's so mild.

 When **Thomas Edison's** son **Charles** ran for governor of New Jersey in 1940, he downplayed his connection to the famous inventor.

"I would not have anyone believe that I am leaning on the name Edison," Charles told a political rally. "I would rather have you know me merely as the result of one of my father's earlier experiments."

When **Thomas Babington, Baron Macaulay** was running for reelection to Parliament, he debated his opponent but was rudely interrupted when a man in the audience hit Macaulay by throwing a dead cat at him.

As Macaulay got back to his feet, the man apologized, explaining that he had thrown the cat at his opponent. "Then I wish you had meant it for me and struck him," Macaulay said.

 A congressman was making a particularly long speech, during which he mentioned that he was "speaking for posterity."

Congressman **Henry Clay** interrupted his colleague to say, "And it seems that you are resolved to keep on speaking until your audience arrives."

In 1955 actor **Zero Mostel** was forced to testify at a televised session of the House Un-American Activities Committee, which was investigating whether Communists had infiltrated showbiz.

Mostel, a Broadway and TV actor whose career was ruined by the long investigation, told the congressmen, "I want to thank the committee for making it possible for me to be on TV, because I've been blacklisted from it for five years."

 When **Richard Nixon** was running for president in 1960, his campaign advisers scheduled him on a whistle-stop train tour of California. At each stop, Nixon would make his stump speech to the crowd from the back plat-form of the train, then ride on to the next town.

But at one stop, the Republican candidate was begin-ning his speech when the train suddenly pulled out of the station. What went wrong? A political operative named **Dick Tuck**, dressed like a railway engineer, had ordered the train to move on. Tuck was a Democrat.

 A different approach to democracy was tried in Sweden in the Middle Ages. Every man who wanted to become the mayor of Hurdenburg put his chin on a large table. A louse was released in the middle of the table. Whichever man's beard the louse chose to run up was mayor for a year.

We do things differently in the United States, where no elected officials are chosen by a louse even if they are one.

 Cordell Hull, who was secretary of state for **Franklin Roosevelt**, learned through his long years in govern-ment service not to make assumptions. One day while traveling on a train through ranching country, Hull's companion looked out the window at a flock of sheep and commented that they had all been sheared.

Glancing at the herd, Hull replied, "Sheared on this side, anyway."

Serious politicians make serious campaign promises they have no intention, or ability, to keep. Wacko candidates run on absurd platforms. The idea of keeping an absurd promise is itself absurd. So either way, the public ends up with the same thing: very, very little.

My favorite absurdist candidate was **Carl LaFong**, who ran for mayor of San Francisco many years ago on the Pastrami Ticket. His campaign platform: "I love pastrami."

That's a platform I could get behind, I thought, especially at the deli. If LaFong got elected, we might have a renaissance of good sandwiches. Whereas whichever serious politician wins is not actually going to lower our taxes, improve our schools, fix the roads, or get us a better lunch. His major achievement will be to come back in a few years and tell us he needs another term to finish the job he didn't do the first time around.

So vote pastrami—unless, of course, you prefer the lesser of two sandwiches: corn beef on rye.

 Adlai Stevenson ran for the White House twice and twice lost to the war hero General **Dwight Eisenhower**. Even in defeat, Stevenson was known for his firm grasp of the economic pitfalls that America would soon face.

"There was a time when a fool and his money were soon parted," Stevenson warned the American people. "But now it happens to everybody."

Democratic senator **Edward Kennedy** was popular in his home state of Massachusetts. But Republican **Ronald Reagan** was even more popular as president. While Kennedy wasn't often on the winning side of Senate votes, he got some revenge by winning the battle of wits.

"Ronald Reagan must love poor people," Kennedy once said, "because he's creating so many more of them."

 When **James Polk** defeated him in a race for the White House, **Millard Fillmore** expressed the view of losers in many elections when he said, "May God save the country, for it's evident that the people will not."

 When President **Calvin Coolidge** declined to seek reelection, a reporter asked him why he wouldn't run again. The president gave him the kind of straightforward evasion that made Coolidge a legend for taciturn commentary: "Because there's no chance for advancement."

 When Senator **Theodore Green** ran for reelection in Rhode Island, he found a simple, money-saving way to secure votes. He stiffed waiters and cab drivers on their tips, then urged them cheerfully to "Vote Republican." Green was a Democrat.

When **Richard Lee** was running for reelection as mayor of New Haven, Connecticut, an angry voter told him, "I wouldn't vote for you if you were Saint Peter."

"If I were Saint Peter," Lee replied, "you wouldn't be in my district."

William Huston Natcher spent forty years in Congress representing the second district of Kentucky. During that time, he set a congressional record by never missing a roll-call vote, no matter how minor the matter. He was yea or nay in 18,401 house votes in a row.

Was he proud of his voting record? So proud he wished he had never started it. His advice to new members of Congress: Miss a vote early in your career so you don't get into the same trap of having to show up just to keep the streak alive.

 When **Ronald Reagan** was elected governor of California, movie mogul **Jack Warner** said, "It's our fault. We should have given him better parts."

 The gifted orator Congressman **Henry Clay** made this noble thought famous: "I had rather be right than be president."

Many years later, when **Thomas Reed** was Speaker of the House of Representatives, he heard Clay's proclamation reiterated by a congressman of a far shallower merit.

"The gentleman need not worry," Reed remarked, "for he will never be either."

For some time after that, congressmen stopped quoting Clay's line in support of their positions.

Before he became president, **Ronald Reagan** didn't need speechwriters to pen his clever retorts. Once while his limousine was edging slowly through a student demonstration, he heard the protestors chanting, "We are the future."

He scribbled a response and held it up to the window. His retort: "I'll sell my bonds."

"All wars are popular for the first thirty days," said diplomat **Arthur Schlesinger Jr**.

Many historians claim that the Roman emperor **Caligula** was mad (or maybe he just wanted to prove that it wasn't so tough to run a government) when the emperor named his favorite horse to the post of consul of the empire.

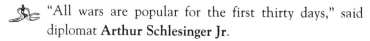

BONUS LAUGH
GEORGE W. BUSH
VS.
THE ENGLISH LANGUAGE

On education: "The illiteracy level of our children are appalling."

More on education: "America is a literate country and a hopefuller country."

On the energy crisis: "We need an energy bill that encourages consumption."

On unemployment: "We want anybody who can find work to be able to find work."

On war: "You disarm or we will."

 On fighting terrorism: "Our enemies are innovative and resourceful, and so are we. They never stop thinking about new ways to harm our country and our people, and neither do we."

 On the world situation: "We spent a lot of time talking about Africa, as we should. Africa is a nation that suffers from incredible disease."

 On the Democrats: "They want the federal government controlling Social Security like it's some kind of federal program."

(Social Security has been some kind of federal program for almost seventy years.)

 On what he believes: "I know what I believe. I will continue to articulate what I believe and what I believe—I believe what I believe is right."

FROM THE JOKE FILE

1. A die-hard Republican finally came to the end of the road. Lying on his deathbed, he beckoned his wife closer. "There's only one thing left that I've got to do before I go," he whispered.

   With tears in her eyes, she said, "What, dear?"

"Switch parties," he said. "Before I die, I want to register as a Democrat."

His wife was shocked. "Have you taken leave of your senses?" she asked. "We've been Republicans all our lives."

"I know," he said. "But wouldn't you rather have one of them die than one of us?"

2. Three politicians went deer hunting and spotted a big buck. The Democrat fired first and missed five feet to the left. The Republican got off the next shot, but he missed five feet to the right. The Independent didn't fire his gun at all. He just averaged the other two together and said, "We got him, boys."

3. Senator **Hillary Clinton** returned from a trip back to Arkansas, leading a pig off the plane.

"Good-looking pig you've got there, Senator," her aide said.

"It's an Arkansas razorback that I got for Bill," Hillary said.

The assistant nodded and said, "Good trade, ma'am."

4. Back in the old days, a man from the deep woods was elected to represent his state in the Senate. Senate rules gave him the right to hire any adviser he wanted at the government's expense.

So the man interviewed every lawyer in his part of the woods and found none smart enough to give him good advice. Then he talked to the businessmen in the state and several college professors, but didn't like any of them well enough to take them to Washington.

Finally, he stopped for the night at the farm of an old friend. The two men debated the issues of the day while the senator helped the farmer with his chores. The senator noticed that every time an issue was raised, the ears on the farmer's jackass would either stand straight up or flop down.

"It's almost like your jackass is listening to our conversation," the senator said.

"Yes, sir, he does that," the farmer said. "The most opinionated jackass I've ever had. Ears up means yes. Ears flopped down means he's against it."

So the senator tested the jackass and found that the animal, unlike his friend, agreed with his position on all the issues. "I'm going to buy that jackass from you," the senator said, "and take him with me to Washington to serve as my adviser."

And that's why jackasses have been holding down all the good-paying government jobs ever since.

WHAT THE PROS SAY

 Comic **Will Rogers:** "The taxpayers are sending congressmen on expensive trips abroad. It might be worth it except they keep coming back."

 Comic **Milton Berle:** "In Washington a man gets up to speak and doesn't say a thing, and the other men disagree with him for three hours."

Writer **P. J. O'Rourke:** "The Republicans are the party that says government doesn't work and then gets elected and proves it."

 Comic **Mort Sahl:** "I've arranged with my executor to be buried in Chicago. Because when I die, I want to still remain active politically."

 Comic **Will Durst:** "Still can't figure out what the outcry over gay marriage is about. I thought the whole idea was to keep gays from having sex. What better way than marriage can you think of to achieve that?"

 Comic **Pat Paulsen:** "A gun is a necessity. Who knows when you're walking down the street and you'll spot a moose?"

 Comic **Rodney Dangerfield:** "I get no respect. The way my luck is running, if I was a politician I would be honest."

 Comic **Bob Hope:** "I love to go to Washington, if only to be near my money."

 Writer **Heywood Broun:** "A liberal is a man who leaves the room when the fight starts."

 Newspaper columnist **Franklin Pierce Adams:** "What this country needs is a good five-cent nickel."

Comic **Mort Sahl:** "Adlai Stevenson dropped in to see my show in San Francisco, and he said, 'You can represent the oppressed majority, the Democrats.'"

 Comic **Will Durst:** "You know why there are no Democrats on *Star Trek*? Because it's set in the future."

 Comic **Bill Maher:** "I think Iraqis feel that if we drove smaller cars, maybe we wouldn't have to kill them for their oil."

 Comic **Dennis Miller:** "President Bush gave his first-ever presidential radio address in both English and Spanish. Reaction was mixed, however, as people were trying to figure out which one was which."

 Writer **P. J. O'Rourke:** "Giving money and power to government is like giving whiskey and car keys to teenage boys."

 Comic **Emo Philips:** "I got a letter from the IRS. Apparently I owe them eight hundred dollars. So I sent them a letter back. I said, 'If you'll remember, I fastened my return with a paper clip, which according to your very own latest government Pentagon spending figures will more than make up for the difference.'"

 Writer **Peter Cook:** "War and nudism do not mix. You've never had a war, ever, started by a nudist."

Cartoonist **Doug Larson:** "Instead of giving a politician the keys to the city, it might be better to change the locks."

 Writer **H. L. Mencken:** "Democracy is a pathetic belief in the collective wisdom of individual ignorance."

 Writer **Will Rogers:** "Congress is good enough for me. They have been writing my material for years."

 Writer **Peter Cook:** "Something went out of my life when Nixon dramatically told the press that they would not have Richard Nixon to kick around anymore. Luckily, he changed his mind and duly returned to be kicked around in the prescribed manner."

 Writer **H. L. Mencken:** "Giving every man a vote has no more made men wise and free than Christianity has made them good."

 Newspaper columnist **Art Buchwald:** "It is believed that the U.S. and the Soviets have stockpiled enough weapons to destroy each other's citizens ten times over. The first step then is to produce an agreement that would reduce the nuclear arsenals in both countries to the point where they could only kill every American and Soviet citizen *five* times."

Nineteenth-century writer **Bill Nye:** "Health journals are now asserting that to maintain a sound constitution you should lie only on the right side. The health journals may mean well enough, but what are you going to do if you are editing a Democratic paper?"

 Comic **Mark Russell:** "The Republicans have a new health-care proposal: Just say *no* to illness!"

 Comic **Mort Sahl:** "Liberals feel unworthy of their possessions. Conservatives feel they deserve everything they've stolen."

 Comic **Vaughn Meader:** "My candidate does not know the meaning of the word *compromise*, does not know the meaning of the word *appeasement*, does not know the meaning of the word *cowardice*—and he's done quite well despite this lousy vocabulary."

 Writer **Nora Ephron:** "As far as the men who are running for president are concerned, they aren't even people I would date."

MY TURN
THE NIGHT SHIFT OF POLITICS

When **Abraham Lincoln** said that you couldn't fool all the people all the time, he left out the political wisdom that you don't have to.

If you can fool 51 percent of the people every four years, you're a winner. That's all it takes. And how hard can that be when you've got a $300 million ad budget?

One thing for certain after a presidential election: Whoever wins, almost half the people lose. They're going to be unhappy because a democracy represents only slightly more than half the people at any one time.

Or we could change the system and have a real democracy. Whoever wins that 51 percent gets to be president 51 percent of the time. The other candidate gets the job 49 percent of the time. It's only fair.

Besides, if we get a fill-in host for the *Tonight Show*, why can't we have a fill-in for America? Some of our presidents are on vacation about half the time anyway—and we're probably better off when they are.

"Mr. President, we've got the premier of Russia on the red phone. He wants to know what you've done to correct that slice in your swing."

"Tell him I'll get back to him as soon as I solve world hunger and finish the back nine."

If our great country can have gas stations and diners that stay open twenty-four hours a day, why can't we have a West Wing that's open for business around the clock?

I figure, the guy who comes in second in the election, he's got to work the night shift.

They keep telling us the president has his eye on the future of the world, not to mention his finger on the button. So we need the very best guy we can get for such a tough job.

I don't buy the hype. How tough a job can it be if you get to set your own office hours and take as much vacation time as you want? And no one complains that you're goofing off most of the time.

Then in your fourth year on the job, you can leave the White House entirely and spend five months on the campaign trail. If your job is so important, Mr. President, how come it makes no difference whether you show up at the office or not?

Most of us have jobs where if we didn't show up for five months, they'd notice.

CHAPTER 12

DOCTORS WITHOUT PANTS, LAWYERS WITHOUT BRIEFS

IN THE FUNNY PROFESSIONS

If 70 percent of the world's lawyers are working in the United States . . .

Sorry, had to run over to the courthouse, where I'm being sued for the pain and suffering caused the legal profession by my telling too many bad lawyer jokes.

Anyway, if doctors have to trade in their Mercedeses for BMWs because the HMOs aren't paying them enough to go, "Hmm, I haven't seen that before" . . .

Sorry, my doctor just phoned to say he was going to sue me for slandering the medical profession—if I survive whatever it is I'm going to get the next time I'm in his office.

Maybe I'd better let the lawyers and doctors tell their own jokes.

IT'S A FUNNY LIFE

 Nineteenth-century businessman **Russell Sage** was considering a lawsuit against a rival, but wasn't sure he could win it. He went to see his attorney and laid out the case.

"It's ironclad," the lawyer said. "We can't possibly lose."

"Then we won't sue," Sage concluded. "I just gave you my opponent's side of the case."

 When **James McNeill Whistler's** dog came down with a mysterious throat ailment, he didn't take him to a vet, but to a prominent throat specialist in London.

The doctor thought it inappropriate for Whistler to ask him to treat a pet, but did so when the famous artist insisted.

Whistler received a message a few days later, requesting him to return to the doctor's office at once. Whistler assumed it was a bad lab report for his dog and rushed over.

The doctor explained that there was nothing wrong with Whistler's pet. He had asked the artist to come to his office to paint his door.

 The night was bitter and chilly as General **Ulysses S. Grant** walked into the lobby of an Illinois hotel, where he joined several lawyers drinking by the fireplace.

One of the lawyers said to Grant, "You look like you've gone through hell to get here."

"That's right," Grant agreed.

"And how did you find things down there?" a second lawyer asked.

"Just like here," Grant said, "lawyers all closest to the fire."

A visitor to **Dr. Albert Schweitzer's** hospital in French Equatorial Africa complained about the extreme heat. Schweitzer said he wouldn't keep a thermometer in the hospital because "if I knew how hot it was, I don't think I would be able to endure it either."

A friend offered Denver judge **Ben Lindsay** a cool drink on a hot day. "Have you ever tried gin and ginger ale?" the friend suggested.

"No," the judge admitted. "But I have often tried fellows who have."

Here's one that doctors hear all the time. In this case it came from Hall of Famer **Mickey Mantle**, long after he had retired from baseball: "If I knew I was going to live this long," Mantle said, "I'd have taken better care of myself."

When eighteenth-century American lawyer **Hugh Brackenridge** was challenged to a duel, he came up with this unique response: "If you want to try your pistols, take some object, a tree or a barn door, about my dimensions. If you hit that, send me word; and I shall acknowledge that if I had been in the same place, you might also have hit me."

BONUS LAUGH
ONE MAN, ONE WOMAN

Legal questions arising from the No Marriage Left Behind Act:

One man and one woman?
Legal. Five cents. Next.

One man and two women?
Illegal, unless sequential. Then legal, but costly.

Two men and one woman?
See above. Plus, laundry issues.

One man and 317 women?
Wrong country. Next.

One man and one tree?
Illegal, unless in preparation for cutting down tree to create logging jobs.

One man and one imaginary woman?
Perfection. Although laundry problems may arise after first week.

How does the new law define marriage?
Marriage is a legal state entered into by all Republicans and any Democrats in their right minds, should any ever arise.

Are there any loopholes in the new law?

A big one. Many people believe that a marriage unites a man and a woman, so that two become one. That unity is declared at the marriage ceremony. Therefore, that new entity would then be legally entitled to marry another union of two-into-one, creating a legal union of four.

One problem—laundry issues again.

FROM THE JOKE FILE

1. Upon meeting her husband's new doctor at a party, a woman complained, "Bill used to be the most wonderful husband and father. But since he went to see you, Bill's become highly critical of me and the children, and I think he's interested in another woman. What did you do to him?"

   "Fit him for contact lenses," the doctor explained.

2. A lawyer was driving down a dark country road when he side-swiped a car driven by a doctor. Seeing the doctor was shaken up, the lawyer offered him a shot of brandy from his pocket flask.

   "Thanks, that steadied me," the doctor said, giving the flask back. "Aren't you going to take a drink?" the doctor asked as the lawyer put the flask away.

   The lawyer shook his head. "No, I think I'll just wait for the police to get here."

WHAT THE PROS SAY

 Comic **Milton Berle:** "My doctor told me that jogging could add years to my life. I think he was right. I feel ten years older already."

 Comic **Steven Wright:** "Ninety-nine percent of lawyers give the rest a bad name."

 Comic **George Carlin:** "Isn't it a bit unnerving that doctors call what they do practice?"

 Comic **Jerry Seinfeld:** "Doctors always want you to take your pants off . . . 'You take your pants off, and then I'll tell you what I think about everything. I speak to no one wearing pants.' It's a little psychological leverage for him. In any difference of opinion, pants always beats no pants."

 Comic **Pat Paulsen:** "More and more people are expressing the view that doctors are charging too much for their services. Now the complaints of exorbitant fees come almost without exception from those who have been going to doctors. I say these people are sick."

 Playwright **Jean Kerr:** "A lawyer is never entirely comfortable with a friendly divorce, any more than a good mortician wants to finish his job and then have the patient sit up on the table."

Comic **Henny Youngman:** "I told the doctor I broke my leg in two places. He told me to quit going to those places."

 Comic **Steve Martin:** "First, the doctor told me the good news: I was going to have a disease named after me."

 Writer **Calvin Trillin:** "If law school is so hard to get through, how come there are so many lawyers?"

 Writer **H. L. Mencken:** "A judge is a law student who marks his own examination papers."

 Comic **Henny Youngman:** "A wonderful doctor gave this guy six months to live. When he couldn't pay his bills, he gave him another six months."

 Writer **Florynce Kennedy:** "I can remember—I was still practicing law at that time—going to court in pants, and the judge's remarking that I wasn't properly dressed. He's sitting there in a long black dress gathered at the yoke, and I said, 'Judge, if you won't talk about what I'm wearing, I won't talk about what you're wearing.'"

 Comic **Pam Stone:** "I had a girlfriend who told me she was in the hospital for female problems. I said, 'Get real! What does that mean?' She said, 'You know, *female* problems.' I said, 'What? You can't parallel park? You can't get credit?'"

Comic **Red Skelton:** "My doctor said I was sound as a dollar. That scared the hell out of me."

 Comic **Jerry Seinfeld:** "Kids could always resolve any dispute by calling it. One of them will say, 'I got the front seat . . . I called it.'

"And the other kid has no recourse. 'He called it. What can I do?'

"If there was a kid court of law, it holds up. 'Your Honor, my client did ask for the front seat.'

"The judge says, 'Did he call it?'

"'Well, no, he didn't call it.'

"He bangs the gavel. 'Objection overruled. He has to call it. Case closed.'"

 Comic **Groucho Marx:** "She got her good looks from her father. He's a plastic surgeon."

 Cowboy comic **Baxter Black:** "Remember when you're signing a contract—the large print giveth and the small print taketh away."

 Writer **Erma Bombeck:** "Never go to a doctor whose office plants have died."

 Comic **Steve Landesberg:** "Honesty is the best policy, but insanity is a better defense."

MY TURN
CRUEL AND
REALLY UNUSUAL PUNISHMENT

Cruel and unusual punishment is prohibited by the Constitution. But who are we kidding? All punishment is cruel.

If they locked you up in a nice hotel suite with room service, cable TV, and a swimming pool, that wouldn't be punishment. It would be the Holiday Inn.

The unusual punishments are even worse than the cruel ones. We've been punishing people for so long, it's pretty hard to find an unusual way to do it.

"First, we're going to put this bag of gumdrops on your foot, the five-hundred-pound bag. Then we'll dye your hair lime green, but only every other hair. Also, you have to watch *Seinfeld* reruns for the next ten to twenty years."

Now that would be unusual punishment.

CHAPTER 13

THE MOBSTER WHO KNEW FISH

AND OTHER OUTLAW COMICS

Most humor is gallows humor because God made us both deadly and laughable—an odd combination.

That's why stand-ups love it when they slay an audience. "I killed out there," they brag afterward, "I murdered 'em." And often, they get away with their crimes.

IT'S A FUNNY LIFE

 Inmates in a Massachusetts penitentiary went on a hunger strike because the food in prison was so bad. And they had one other complaint—they weren't given seconds.

Mark Twain went fishing in Maine out of season. The writer did so well, he bragged about his catch to a stranger he met in a bar that night.

After the writer told his new drinking companion about all the fish he'd caught, the man said, "Well, friend, I'm the state game warden. Who are you?"

"To be perfectly truthful, warden," Twain replied, "I'm the biggest liar in the whole United States."

 Before he became rich and famous, the French writer **Honoré de Balzac** struggled to sell his stories and novels, living the meager life of a starving writer.

One night he woke up to find a burglar picking the lock on his writing desk. Instead of attacking the burglar, Balzac laughed at him.

"Why are you laughing?" the surprised thief asked.

The writer shrugged. "To think what risks you take to try to find money in a desk by night where the legal owner can never find any by day."

 What's at stake during the world pipe-smoking championships, sponsored by the International Association of Pipe Smokers Clubs? More than you might think from all the huffing and puffing.

Consider the words of one winner, **Paul Spaniola** of Michigan, who said, "If everybody smoked a pipe, we feel there would never be wars. You'll notice in the newspapers or on TV or in the movies, you never see a hardened violent criminal smoking a pipe."

 Illinois police suspected an inside job when a packet of confiscated marijuana vanished from an evidence cage under their guard. But it wasn't taken by anyone from the department. Investigators finally found the culprit— a mouse that ate the pot.

They were able to identify the suspect because he was the mouse with the big grin on his face.

 Ever wonder what mobsters do for a hobby? Take crime syndicate leader **Sam Giancana**, who favored fishing for relaxation. He also had some smart advice for the fish: If they didn't want to get caught, they should keep their big mouths shut.

 Even the would-be burglar had to admit it was a dumb crime. That realization came upon him suddenly when he broke in through the rear door of a restaurant in 1957 to steal the night's receipts.

Once inside, he found it wasn't after hours after all. The place was still open for business. All the employees and customers were staring at the burglar as he stood there with a crowbar in his hand and the police on the way to arrest him.

Luckily for the crook, he had better luck in his next career, as a country singer, for it was **Merle Haggard** going through a major change of heart.

An inmate on death row came up with a unique plan to avoid the electric chair. He ate so much that he gained a huge amount of weight in an attempt to convince the warden that he wouldn't fit in the chair. Didn't work.

 In 1983 two thieves broke into a London post office and stole several sacks of mail. To make sure the postal clerk couldn't call the police before they made their getaway, the thieves glued her to the wall.

 The old *Sacramento Union* newspaper, now out of business, used to supplement its street sales and advertising revenue with **Mark Twain's** desk.

The paper liked to bill itself as "Mark Twain's Newspaper" because America's favorite writer had once written its travel stories. When the paper's editors found a collector, they would sell him Twain's battered old writing desk. And when they found another collector, they'd also sell him Twain's battered old writing desk.

In an old newspaper, there is no shortage of old, battered desks.

 Think no-smoking sections are unfair? In parts of Germany in the seventeenth century, smoking was considered a crime punishable by death. If the tobacco didn't kill you, the tobacco police would.

BONUS LAUGH
TOO MANY MASTERMINDS

I've thought about becoming the next **James Bond**. But I've decided to turn the job down.

I feel it's okay to save the world once. But if you have to turn around and save it all over again year after year, eventually you will have to face the hard reality that you're in a rut. You'll never have to stop saving this world.

As a world, we simply refuse to learn our lesson. There's always some bright, up-and-coming megalomaniac who thinks: I know all the other megalomaniacs couldn't stop Bond, but I have a foolproof plan. I'll get about five hundred guys to shoot at him. Odds are someone's going to hit him.

Oh, you fool. They never learn, these world beaters. You've got to give these guys target practice *before* you turn them loose on Bond.

As for me taking over the Bond job, sorry, life's too short. After the tenth or eleventh time, saving the world just seems so—oh no, not again. Been there, saved that.

I've often wondered: What exactly do all these criminal masterminds want with this world? None of them have a clue what they'd do with it once they got it. Would you want to get stuck running the interstate highway system or the post office? Big headaches there.

Anyway, I feel the world is safe enough without my help. As Bond—James Bond—put it, "We don't have to worry about the morons taking over the world. The idiots will never let them."

FROM THE JOKE FILE

1. A cop pulled over a car for speeding. The officer drew his gun when he saw that the driver had five Bowie knives on the seat next to him. "What are those for?" he demanded.

   "I'm a juggler," the driver reassured the policeman. "I use the knives in my act."

   "Prove it," the cop said.

   The driver got out of the car and started juggling the big knives, until he had all five in the air at the same time.

   As another car passed them, the second driver turned to his buddy and said, "I've got to stop drinking. Look at the sobriety test they make you do now."

2. "Did you get another ticket for speeding?"

   "No, this one was for driving too slow."

   "Cops don't give tickets for that."

   "Sure they do. If he hadn't caught me, I never would have gotten the ticket."

3. When the jury came in with an innocent verdict, the judge blew his top, knowing the evidence had proven the suspect guilty.

> "On what possible grounds could you call the defendant inno-
> cent?" the judge demanded.
>
> "Insanity," explained the jury foreman.
>
> The judge looked at the jury as they all nodded in agree-
> ment. "My God," he cried, "all twelve of you?"

WHAT THE PROS SAY

Comic **Pat Paulsen:** "There are large numbers who oppose gambling on moral grounds. And many of their arguments sound pretty convincing. But on closer inspection we find out that these same people are also opposed to robbery, blackmail, and murder. Some people will knock anything."

Comic **George Carlin:** "If someone with multiple personalities threatens to kill himself, is it considered a hostage situation?"

Comic **Jan Murray:** "They hijacked a bus filled with Japanese tourists. But, thank God, they got over two million pictures of the hijackers."

Comic **Ronnie Corbett:** "A cement truck collided with a prison van. Motorists are asked to be on the lookout for sixteen hardened criminals."

Writer **Ellen Cleghorne:** "When this judge let a rapist go because the woman had been wearing a miniskirt and so was 'asking for it,' I thought, Ladies, what we all should do is this: Next time we see an ugly guy on the street, shoot him. After all, he knew he was ugly when he left the house. He was asking for it."

Comic **Jerry Seinfeld:** "Like the WANTED posters at the post office . . . Why don't they just hold on to this guy when they're taking his picture? The guy's there with you."

Comic **Norm Crosby:** "When you go into court you are putting your fate into the hands of twelve people who weren't smart enough to get out of jury duty."

Comic **Bill Maher:** "Things aren't right. If a burglar breaks into your home and you shoot him, he can sue you. For what, restraint of trade?"

Comic **Emo Philips:** "I was pulled over in Massachusetts for reckless driving. When brought before the judge, I was asked if I knew what the punishment for drunk driving in that state was. I said, 'I don't know . . . reelection to the Senate?'"

Comic **Dennis Miller:** "A recent police study found that you're much more likely to get shot by a fat cop if you run."

Comic **Robin Williams:** "We had gay burglars the other night. They broke in and rearranged the furniture."

Writer **Will Rogers:** "The toughest part of robbing nowadays is to find somebody that has something."

 Comic **Steven Wright:** "Curiosity killed the cat, but for a while I was a suspect."

 Writer **Mark Twain:** "Murder is always a mistake. One should never do anything that one cannot talk about after dinner."

 Comic **Jerry Seinfeld:** "The only thing dumber than the helmet is the helmet law, the point of which is to protect a brain that is functioning so poorly, it's not even trying to stop the cracking of the head that it's in."

 Comic **Mark Russell:** "The criminality in question, defined by the court, is sodomy, taken from the ancient city of Sodom. You can still commit Gomorrah."

 Writer **Kin Hubbard:** "It would be a swell world if everybody was as pleasant as the fellow who's trying to skin you."

 Writer **Peter Cook:** "[An Identi-Kit is] when you piece together the appearance of the face of the criminal. Unfortunately, we're not able to piece together the face of the criminal. I wish we could. Once you have captured the criminal's face, the other parts of the criminal's body are not too far behind, being situated immediately below the criminal's face."

Writer **Will Rogers:** "One day there were four innocent people shot here in New York . . . Hard to find four innocent people in New York, even if you don't shoot them."

 Comic **Elayne Boosler:** "I have six locks on my door all in a row. When I go out, I lock every other one. I figure no matter how long somebody stands there picking the locks, they are always locking three."

 Comic **Victor Borge:** "My great-grandfather invented the burglar alarm. Unfortunately, it was stolen from him."

MY TURN
THE ONLY EQUAL OPPORTUNITY EMPLOYER

That would be crime, of course. No unions, no licenses, no experience necessary.

As for those of us who more or less play by the rules, we'll never solve the problem of crime because our laws are made by politicians, whose sympathies are naturally with the criminal class.

No one gets far in politics without the nerve of a thief and the craft of a con man—unless you're running for president, when all past crimes are washed clean as youthful indiscretions. If Richard Nixon was not a crook, then no other prisoner of the White House was either.

We can't depend on the cops and the lawyers to clean up the criminal element because their living depends on the hard work of crooks. If all the crooks went on strike, what would the cops and the DA do? Set up a counter–picket line?

The only way to get rid of crime is to make everything legal. We'd have just as much criminal-type activity, but a lot less guilt weighing us down.

When everything is legal, there will be no more criminal behavior. We'd say, Sure, he's a drug dealer, but he pays his taxes like all the other businessmen in town. You know Joe, used to be a car mechanic. But after rehab, he became a car thief. Saves us a lot of money too. It's cheaper to pay the insurance than it is the repairs.

CHAPTER 14

THE PLATINUM BIKINI

AND OTHER CRIMES OF FASHION

When high heels were invented during the Renaissance, they were worn by men from the upper class who wanted to assume a position of superiority over other men.

These wobbly elitists soon found there was one problem with the high life: They kept falling off their heels. Hard to feel superior when you're stumbling around and falling down at every other step.

So men passed high heels on to upper-class women, who wore them proudly to demonstrate that they were too rich to walk.

The world of fashion has been providing us with laughs ever since.

IT'S A FUNNY LIFE

 Judith Martin, famed for her syndicated **Miss Manners** newspaper column, received a letter from a reader asking, "Dear Miss Manners: What is the correct way to walk in high-heeled shoes?"

Her reply? "Gentle Reader: Left, right, left, right, left, right."

 Politician **Jill Ruckelshaus** points out the absurdity of one of society's long-standing conventions: how people are allowed to dance.

"It occurred to me when I was thirteen and wearing white gloves and Mary Janes and going to dancing school," she said, "that no one should have to dance backward all their lives."

 Look at the magazine rack and you'll see enough fashion and beauty magazines to give every woman in the world something to read while waiting for her beautician to work miracles. There couldn't possibly be a group of women without their own specialized fashion magazine— could there?

There was in 2001, when a Dutch publisher brought out *Mainline Lady,* a fashion magazine designed for the upscale female drug addict.

Mainline Lady gave makeup, clothing, and dating advice to women trying to balance the dual demands of getting high and looking great at the same time.

John Christie, a wealthy Englishman in the early 1900s, thought he could save a lot of money by buying personal items in bulk, including a consignment of two thousand dancing shoes, although it is unlikely any one person could ever dance that much.

In style, you've seen people who have it and people who don't. But you may not have known that a sense of fashion divided along party lines.

Let Democrat **Willie Brown**, the ex-mayor of San Francisco, put you straight: "Dressing is a matter of taste," he said, "and I've met very few Republicans with good taste."

Mormon leader **Brigham Young** was shocked by a new nineteenth-century fad and denounced it from the pulpit as an improper way for men to dress. What got him so upset? Men's pants made with that new-fangled button fly.

In 1977 Miss United Kingdom came up with a unique idea for the Miss World contest. She entered the swimsuit contest wearing a platinum bikini. It cost ten thousand dollars. Despite her investment in the spectacular, she didn't even win the talent contest.

During a press conference, a reporter commented that famed lawyer **Clarence Darrow** didn't appear to be ready for court because his suit was rumpled and cheap-looking.

"I pay more for my clothes than any of you," Darrow countered. "The only difference is that you probably don't sleep in yours."

 When **Priscilla Presley** was married to **Elvis**, she had not only one of the richest men in America but one of the tallest bouffant hairdos, too.

When Elvis gave her a Corvair, Priscilla and her hair wouldn't fit in the driver's seat. She had to drive with her hair tilted out the window.

 In the 1960s, Cadillac promised that the seats in its luxury cars were so plush you could roll around on them in your mink coat without damaging the fur. To prove it, they had women in minks roll around on the seats of test Caddies, then demonstrate that their fur was fine.

In the 1970s, when jeans manufacturers realized they could sell designer jeans for a premium price, two of the most successful marketing schemes were sold under the designer labels **Jordache** and **Gloria Vanderbilt**.

There were no such designers. The "Jordache" name was chosen for its Frenchness. Gloria Vanderbilt, at least, was an actual person. She was chosen because she came from a wealthy society family, not because she could design fancy jeans. Her contribution: her signature stitched on buyers' butts.

FROM THE JOKE FILE

1. A fashion model who was down on her luck prayed to God, "Help me, Lord. I'm broke. I haven't gotten a modeling job in months, and my agent dropped me. Please let me win the lottery."

   But she lost. The next week, she prayed to God again, "Help me, Lord. I've been thrown out of my apartment. My car was repossessed, and my beautician says if I don't pay my bill, I'll never look pretty again. God, please let me win the lottery."

   But her luck was still bad, and she lost again. Finally, she prayed, "Lord, why have you forsaken me? I've lost everything. Please, let me win the lottery just one time so I can have a second chance in life."

   Suddenly, she heard the voice of God talking to her from the heavens. "Work with me, babe," God said. "Buy a ticket."

2. "I've been feeling so blue for days," Heather told her friend. "Can't seem to shake the feeling."

   "Do what I do," Laura said. "Whenever I'm down in the dumps, I buy myself some new clothes."

   "Oh," Heather said, "I was wondering where you got them."

WHAT THE PROS SAY

 Comic *Jerry Seinfeld:* "Where lipstick is concerned, the important thing is not color, but to accept God's final word on where your lips end."

 Comic *Joan Rivers:* "I was dating a transvestite. My mother said, 'Marry him. You'll double your wardrobe.'"

 Poet *Jean Cocteau:* "Art produces ugly things which frequently become beautiful with time. Fashion, on the other hand, produces beautiful things which always become ugly with time."

 Writer *Mark Twain:* "Clothes make the man. Naked people have little or no influence on society."

 Writer *Oscar Wilde:* "Fashion is a form of ugliness so intolerable that we have to alter it every six months."

 Comic *Jerry Seinfeld:* "The idea behind the tuxedo is the woman's point of view that men are all the same, so we might as well dress them that way. That's why a wedding is like the joining together of a beautiful, glowing bride and some guy . . . So in case the groom chickens out, everybody just takes one step over, and she marries the next guy. That's why it's not 'Do you take Bob?' but 'Do you take this man?'"

Comic **George Gobel:** "Did you ever feel like the whole world was a tuxedo and you were a pair of brown shoes?"

 Writer **Mary Daly:** "Women's minds have been mutilated and muted to such a state that 'Free Spirit' has been branded into them as a brand name for girdles and bras."

 Comic **Gilda Radner:** "I base my fashion taste on what doesn't itch."

 Comic **Allan Sherman:** "What does God wear, a Pierre Cardin suit?"

 Comic **Jerry Seinfeld:** "Once had a leather jacket that got ruined in the rain. Why does moisture ruin leather? Aren't cows outside a lot of the time? When it's raining, do cows go up to the farmhouse: 'Let us in! We're all wearing leather! Open the door! We're going to ruin the whole outfit here!'"

MY TURN
A PASSION FOR FASHION

Be sure to read the *Washington Post* Style-Setter Section's three-part series "How to Look Your Best While Trying to Come Up with Impossible Solutions to Impossible Problems."

Here are three excerpts from this award-winning series, illustrated by tall, slender fashion models pretending to be short, fat reporters.

1. We can eliminate unemployment just in time to start on that new fall wardrobe.

   Once our corporations send all of our jobs overseas, we will create full employment by 2010—in China.

   In that year every man, woman, and Chinese child will be happily employed or else working fifteen-hour days to handcraft little plastic toys for happy Americans' happy hamburger meals.

2. Let's increase office productivity with a stylish designer clock.

   There's simply not enough time in the eight-hour day for ten of the beautiful people to do the work of the one hundred out-of-step people who were laid off. But today's smart manager can double the output of today's frightened employees while still reducing costs.

   From now on, nine to five will actually take place from seven to eleven. How? By counting each hour on the job as half an hour.

   Under current industry standards, people who are supposed to be working actually perform all sorts of non-work-related activities like breathing, thinking, and worse.

   Why should companies pay people to say hello to each other every day? Wasn't one hello enough?

   Moving from place to place, going to the bathroom, yawning—these are personal activities that should be done on personal time.

3.   Let's colonize the moon with a newer, slimmer you.

Why should we waste billions of tax dollars to send people into space when there are so many things we can waste our money on right here on Earth?

We need a brighter, lighter way to fund space travel, without using dumpy, old-fashioned tax money. Trendy us! We've got it: sell charter memberships to the Lunar Instant Weight-Loss Clinic.

The entire moon colony will be populated by people who feel overweight—and, frankly, who doesn't?

Trendsetters waste billions every year on diet food, diet supplements, and diet gym memberships (just like a regular gym membership, only you use it one-third less).

At our new diet lunar colony, everybody is guaranteed to lose eighty pounds the instant they arrive on the moon. If you weigh two hundred too many pounds here on Earth, you'll automatically drop to a svelte 115 on the moon.

Eat what you like. Never exercise. Take it off and keep it off, only on the moon. Lunatics only need apply.

CHAPTER 15

HALF THE PEOPLE ARE DOING IT

SINFUL LAUGHS

"When authorities warn you of the sinfulness of sex, there is an important lesson to be learned," *The Simpsons* creator **Matt Groening** pointed out: "Do not have sex with the authorities."

We live in a time when one person's sin is the next person's hobby. So let he who is without sin cast the first joke.

IT'S A FUNNY LIFE

 In 1975 the mayor of Oliastro, on the isle of Corsica, tried to rid his town of nude sunbathers. He had any tourists found naked on the beaches arrested and their bodies painted completely blue—an original reinterpretation of the city's blue laws.

🐌 Movie star **Bette Davis** had a jaundiced view of most things because she'd learned the lessons of life from Hollywood. "The act of sex," she said, "gratifying as it may be, is God's joke on humanity."

🐌 Voluptuous movie star **Mae West** had a different opinion of the world's favorite indoor sport. West not only starred in her own sexy movies, but wrote them too, most of them based on her own risqué life. "I've been in more laps," she once said, "than a napkin."

🐌 In the 1950s most baseball managers kept curfew for the players when they were on a road trip and would hit them with a fine if a player wasn't back in his hotel room by an early hour.

Why the curfew? To keep the players away from women. At the time, an unpopular belief held that playing the field weakened players' ability to perform on the field.

New York Yankees manager **Casey Stengel** had a different view on the matter. "Being with a woman all night never hurt no professional baseball player," Casey said. "It's staying up all night looking for a woman that does him in."

Cowboy movie star **Gene Autry** projected an image as wholesome as any that Hollywood fed the movie-loving public. But that didn't mean Autry was unaware of how things worked in showbiz.

Years after he retired from the big screen, Autry commented, "Today you see girls doing on the screen what they used to do off the screen to get on screen."

 A history of the whispers of love between men and women would make a fascinating book, but the research would be tricky to gather.

History does record the sweet nothings that the Roman emperor **Caligula** was prone to whisper to his wife when making romantic advances. "Off comes this head," he would say, kissing her, "whenever I give the word."

Suspicion is that Mrs. Caligula had relatively few headaches.

 A woman wrote to **Dear Abby** asking if birth control pills were deductible on her income tax.

Abby had a simple reply: "Only if they don't work."

But Dear Abby was not alone offering good advice to the sexlorn. Advice columnist **Judith Martin**, known in the trade as **Miss Manners**, tackled this tough question from a reader:

"Dear Miss Manners: What can you do after accidentally calling your present lover by your former lover's name?

"Gentle Reader: Seek a future lover. Such a mistake is easy to do and impossible to undo. Why do you think the term *darling* was invented?"

 During the years that **Winston Churchill** led England, sodomy was on the books as a crime. But Churchill explained that it was nearly impossible to get a jury to convict anyone of the crime because "half the people can't believe it, and half are doing it."

 Movie star **Tallulah Bankhead** liked to party even more than your typical Hollywood enthusiast. When friends tried to get her to stop using cocaine before she got addicted, Tallulah reassured them that cocaine couldn't be habit-forming because she'd been using it for years.

 In the early 1800s when **John Marshall** was chief justice of the Supreme Court, he instituted a rule that none of the justices could touch a drink unless it was raining.

One day after a long court session, Marshall asked one of the other justices to look out the window and see if it was raining. When he reported that there was not a cloud in sight, Marshall responded, "You forget that our jurisdiction is as broad as this republic; and, by the laws of nature, it must be raining someplace in our jurisdiction. Waiter, bring on the rum."

 Not everyone who lives in Las Vegas makes their livelihood off gambling. Some people lose their livelihood to gambling.

Then there was the staff of a Vegas hospital who were found running a gambling syndicate in 1980. They were wagering on which patients would die next.

 Know someone with a gambling problem? Odds are they haven't reached the obsessive level of Britain's **Lord Arlington**, who once bet $400,000 on which raindrop would slide to the bottom of a window first.

FROM THE JOKE FILE

1. Baxter staggered out of the bar and stumbled into identical twins dressed in identical outfits. "I'm drunker than I thought," he said.

    "You're not seeing things, silly," one of the women said. "We really are twins."

    "All four of you?" Baxter shouted.

2. An aging Romeo came up to a pretty girl in a bar and asked, "So where have you been all my life?"

    She looked him over and said, "Well, for the first half of it, I wasn't even born."

WHAT THE PROS SAY

 Writer **Woody Allen:** "The only difference between sex and death is with death you can do it alone and nobody's going to make fun of you."

Comic **George Carlin:** "The main reason Santa is so jolly is because he knows where all the bad girls live."

 Comic **Pat Paulsen:** "Many people today advocate the teaching of . . . you know what . . . in our public schools. A recent nationwide survey disclosed that already 40 percent of our high school boys and girls are receiving this education. However, only 2 percent are receiving it in the classroom."

 Comic **Steve Martin:** "I believe that sex is one of the most beautiful, natural, wholesome things that money can buy."

 Comic **Bob Hope:** "My father told me all about the birds and the bees. The liar. I went steady with a woodpecker till I was twenty-one."

 Comic **Groucho Marx**: "Whoever named it necking was a poor judge of anatomy."

 Writer **Woody Allen:** "There are two types of people in this world: good and bad. The good sleep better, but the bad seem to enjoy the waking hours much more."

 Comic **Spike Milligan:** "Contraceptives should be used on every conceivable occasion."

 Comic **Jerry Seinfeld:** "What is a date, really, but a job interview that lasts all night? The only difference between a date and a job interview is that in not many job interviews is there a chance you'll end up naked at the end of it."

Comic **George Burns:** "Happiness? A good meal, a good cigar, and a good woman. Or a bad woman. It depends on how much happiness you can handle."

 Poet **W. B. Yeats:** "The most unpleasant thing about him is that when he isn't drunk, he's sober."

 Writer **P. J. O'Rourke:** "Anyway, no drug, not even alcohol, causes the fundamental ills of society. If we're looking for the source of our troubles, we shouldn't test people for drugs, we should test them for stupidity, ignorance, greed, and love of power."

 Movie star and writer **Mae West:** "Between two evils I always pick the one I never tried before."

 Comic **Henny Youngman:** "If you're going to do something tonight that you'll be sorry for tomorrow morning, sleep late."

 Newspaper columnist **Helen Rowland:** "Nothing can exceed the grace and tenderness with which men make love—in novels—except the offhand commonplaceness with which they do it in real life."

 Movie star and writer **Mae West:** "When women go wrong, men go right after them."

 Seventeenth-century writer **Hannah Woolley:** "The right Education of the Female Sex, as it is in a manner everywhere neglected, so it ought to be generally lamented. Most in this depraved later Age think a Woman learned and wise enough if she can distinguish her Husband's Bed from another's."

 Writer **Sholom Aleichem:** "A bachelor is a man who comes to work each morning from a different direction."

 Writer **James Kincaid:** "[Teachers] become progressively less thinkable as sexual partners as the students get older and more capable of thinking that sexual partners are what they'd like to have. By junior high it's a mockery, by high school preposterous. Graduate education is an exposure to full-scale, god-awful revulsion; it's a wonder the highly educated propagate."

 Comic **Dick Cavett:** "The bride was pregnant. So at the wedding, everyone threw puffed rice."

 Comic **Graham Chapman:** "I object to all this sex on the television. I mean, I keep falling off."

 Comic **Steve Martin:** "There is one thing I would break up over and that is if she caught me with another woman. I wouldn't stand for that."

 Writer **George Bernard Shaw:** "Why should we take advice on sex from the Pope? If he knows anything about it, he shouldn't."

 Comic **Dennis Miller:** "Guilt is the reason they put the articles in *Playboy*."

Writer **William Burroughs:** "A homosexual can be conditioned to react sexually to a woman, or to an old boot, for that matter. In fact, both homo- and heterosexual experimental subjects have been conditioned to react sexually to an old boot, and you can save a lot of money that way."

 Magazine columnist **Robert Benchley:** "I know I'm drinking myself to a slow death, but then I'm in no hurry."

 Nineteenth-century lecturer **Josh Billings:** "Life is short, but it's long enough to ruin any man who wants to be ruined."

 TV comic **Johnny Carson:** "I know a man who gave up smoking, drinking, sex, and rich food. He was healthy right up to the day he killed himself."

 Comic **W. C. Fields:** "If I had to live my life over, I'd live over a saloon."

 Comic **George Burns:** "It only takes one drink to get me loaded. Trouble is, I can't remember if it's the thirteenth or the fourteenth."

 Comic **Joe E. Lewis:** "You're not drunk if you can lie on the floor without holding on."

 Comic **Chris Rock:** "I don't get high, but sometimes I wish I did. That way, when I messed up in life I would have an excuse. But right now there's no rehab for stupidity."

 Writer **James Thurber:** "One martini is all right. Two are too many, and three are not enough."

Writer **P. J. O'Rourke:** "Marijuana is self-punishing. It makes you acutely sensitive and, in this world, what worse punishment could there be?"

 Comic **Robin Williams:** "Cocaine is God's way of saying you're making too much money."

 Comic **Paula Poundstone:** "The wages of sin are death, but by the time taxes are taken out, it's just sort of a tired feeling."

 Writer **P. J. O'Rourke:** "It's just not fun to have exciting thrills when you're scared. Take the heroes of *The Iliad*, for instance. They really had some exciting thrills, and were they scared? No. They were drunk."

 Writer **Steve Allen:** "I used to be a heavy gambler. But now I just make mental bets. That's how I lost my mind."

MY TURN
PURITAN DATING

The sexy movie star **Mae West** was once asked how she knew so much about men. "I went to night school," she explained.

School records show that Mae got an A in the class.

Another woman who won her A, **Hester Prynne**, wasn't so proud of her accomplishment, according to all reports. We read about Hester in that book called *The Scarlet Letter*, although I believe its original title was *If I Had to Read This Drudge in School, You Have to Read It Too*.

What that book failed to explain was how popular Hester was with all the Puritan men for wearing that big A on her dress. Helped the guys figure out where to go for a date on Saturday night.

CHAPTER 16

IN THE NON-GALLERY OF NON-ART

HANGING OUT WITH THE ARTISTS AND WRITERS

Movie mogul **Sam Goldwyn** didn't like one of the film scripts sent up for his review, so he told the writer, "Let's have some new clichés."

That's the challenge writers face: other people with big ideas. Writers and artists have enough trouble making their own ideas work, which is why they are always so close to an outbreak of absurdity.

IT'S A FUNNY LIFE

 Most struggling writers take a plaintive tone when they submit unsolicited stories to magazines. Not **Erle Stanley Gardner**, who later struck it rich with his Perry Mason courtroom series.

When he was just starting out in the business, Gardner sent a mystery story to a magazine. "'Three o'Clock in the Morning' is a damned good story," he wrote to the editor. "If you have any comments, write them on the back of a check."

 When a friend scolded **Henri de Toulouse-Lautrec** for drinking too much, the French painter countered, "I do not drink so much. I only drink very little, very often."

 Writer **Victor Hugo** was a man of few words, unless he was being paid for them. After his novel *The Hunchback of Notre Dame* was released, Hugo sent a less-than-one-word letter to his publisher to find out how sales were going: "?"

His publisher sent back an equally terse response: "!"

 Pablo Picasso was accustomed to complaints that his portraits weren't realistic because his abstracts didn't look like the people who posed for them.

One disgruntled American collector said he preferred photography to paintings because photos showed what was really there. To prove it, he handed Picasso a photo of his girlfriend.

"Is she really that small?" the artist asked.

 A writer complained to the editor **William Dean Howells** that even though his books were making money, his new writing was not as good as his older work.

"Nonsense," Howells countered. "You write as well as you ever did, but your taste is improving."

 The writer **F. Scott Fitzgerald** and his daring wife, **Zelda**, were notorious among East Coast society in the 1920s for their weekend parties, where hosts and guests competed in outrageous, drunken behavior.

Finally, Scott and Zelda came up with a house rule they hoped would calm things down: "Weekend guests are respectfully notified that invitations to stay over Monday, issued by the host and hostess during the small hours of Sunday morning, must not be taken seriously."

 When British prime minister **Winston Churchill** began painting, a friend asked why his canvases were always landscapes, never portraits. "A tree never complains that I haven't done it justice," Churchill explained.

 One of **James Thurber's** fans gave the *New Yorker* writer the left-handed compliment that his books were even funnier in French. "Yes," Thurber agreed, "I lost something in the original."

 Conceptual artist **Terry Fugate** announced the opening of a show at a new Manhattan gallery. When art critics and collectors showed up at the fashionable midtown address for the gallery opening, they found no art, no gallery—no such building.

The *New York Times* reviewed Fugate's hoax, calling it a "non-gallery of non-art."

 The witty writer **Oscar Wilde** was asked by a British newspaper to list the one hundred best books of all time. Wilde declined, explaining, "I fear it would be impossible because I have written only five."

 New York newspaper columnist **Franklin Pierce Adams** and *New Yorker* writer **Alexander Woollcott** did much of their best work outside the pages of their publications. They were often at their wittiest sitting around the Algonquin round table at lunch.

Upon publication of one of his books, Woollcott mused to the literary crowd at the table, "Ah, what is so rare as a Woollcott first edition?"

Adams shot back, "A Woollcott second edition."

 Writers and artists never stop looking for inspiration. Most find it while awake, but not Italian writer **Gabriele D'Annunzio**. He found his inspiration at night in bed, resting his head on a unique pillow, one he filled with clippings from the hair of his many lovers.

 French painter **Marcel Duchamp** joined the avant-garde group of artists known as the *bata* movement. As part of their performance art, Duchamp would invite people who came to his gallery openings to destroy his paintings with axes. Future collectors did not appreciate the existential gesture.

 Writer **Ernest Hemingway** was notorious in literary circles for challenging friends and enemies to boxing matches. He also favored unusual bets.

Hemingway won a bet with writer **John O'Hara** by breaking O'Hara's walking stick over his own head. This may have been O'Hara's way of getting out of having to spar with Hemingway.

 British writer **John Galsworth** was trying to finish a novel, but kept getting interrupted by a constant stream of idle visitors with time on their hands.

When Galsworth could find no peace and quiet in his own home, he devised a unique scheme to finish his book. He got himself thrown in jail, where, at last, visitors left him alone.

 When **Honoré de Balzac** was a young writer in Paris, he was too poor to furnish his garret. Instead, he decorated the bare flat with words. "Gobelin tapestry with Venetian mirror," he wrote upon the wall. "Picture by Raphael."

When Balzac finally struck it rich with his novels, he spent a fortune to replace his words with the actual treasures.

 Inspiration is hard to find for some writers. Poet **Hart Crane** found a routine that worked for him: First he would insult a friend, then break a few pieces of furniture, then listen to Ravel's *Bolero*. That aroused the muse, and Crane could settle down at last and write a poem.

BONUS LAUGH
COMICS ON COMEDY

Why do we laugh? Obviously, not because people ask us why we laugh.

Even comedians and comic writers may not know why they're able to make people laugh. But that's okay as long as they know how.

 Comic **Lenny Bruce:** "All my humor is based upon destruction and despair. If the whole world were tranquil, without disease and violence, I'd be standing on the bread line right in back of J. Edgar Hoover."

 Comic **Will Rogers:** "Everything is funny as long as it is happening to someone else."

Screenwriter **Mel Brooks:** "Tragedy is when I cut my finger. Comedy is when you fall into an open sewer and die."

Writer **Will Rogers:** "I didn't know whether they were laughing with me or agin me, but so long as they laughed and didn't throw things, I had no kick coming."

Comic **Elayne Boosler:** "In America people become comics because we don't have bullfighting."

Comic **Steve Martin:** "Chaos in the midst of chaos isn't funny, but chaos in the midst of order is."

Cartoonist **Doug Larson:** "A pun is the lowest form of humor, unless you thought of it yourself."

Writer **Robert Benchley:** "In Milwaukee last month a man died laughing over one of his own jokes. That's what makes it so tough for us outsiders. We have to fight home competition."

Writer **E. B. White:** "Analyzing humor is like dissecting a frog. Few people are interested, and the frog dies of it."

FROM THE JOKE FILE

Pete was an illustrator in an ad agency, but he wanted to be a painter. Being a gambler by nature, he quit his job and moved to

Las Vegas, where he opened a gallery to sell his paintings of celebrities to tourists.

Unfortunately, not enough tourists bought his paintings, so Pete ran out of money and took a regular job in a Vegas ad agency. "I swore I'd never work another nine-to-five job, but I had to take this one," he told a friend.

"Was the job that good?" his friend asked.

"No, it was terrible," Pete said, "but I liked the odds."

WHAT THE PROS SAY

 Writer **Somerset Maugham:** "There are three rules for writing a novel. Unfortunately, no one knows what they are."

 Writer **Tom Clancy:** "The difference between fiction and reality? Fiction has to make sense."

 Nineteenth-century lecturer **Josh Billings:** "About the most originality that any writer can hope to achieve honestly is to steal with good judgment."

 Writer **Robert Benchley:** "You have no idea how many problems an author has to face during those feverish days when he is building a novel, and you have no idea how he solves them. Neither has he."

Writer **Mark Twain:** "The difference between literature and journalism is that journalism is unreadable and literature is unread."

 Playwright **Jean Kerr:** "I remember [a playwright] who was carted right back to Menninger's because, at the climactic moment of his play, the bit player who had to call for the police cried out loudly and clearly, 'Help! There's been a murder—call the poloose!'"

 Writer **Shirley Jackson:** "'Age?' she asked. 'Sex? Occupation?'
"'Writer,' I said.
"'Housewife,' she said.
"'Writer,' I said.
"'I'll just put down housewife,' she said."

 Writer **Fran Lebowitz:** "Contrary to what many of you might imagine, a career in letters is not without its drawbacks—chief among them the unpleasant fact that one is frequently called upon to actually sit down and write."

 Newspaper editors have their idiosyncrasies because by the time they get to be editors they've had to put up with the idiosyncrasies of previous editors.

New York *Tribune* editor **Horace Greeley** insisted that the word *news* was plural. "Are there any news?" he once demanded of a reporter.

"Not a new," the reporter replied.

Writer **Fred Allen:** "I can't understand why a person will take a year to write a novel when he can easily buy one for a few dollars."

 Writer **Louis Menand:** "Bourbon has other advantages. A glass or two neat is as close as most people can get to feeling like a novelist or Abstract Expressionist without having to actually write or paint anything—a state thought desirable even by novelists and painters."

 British novelist **Israel Zangwill:** "The way [playwright] George Bernard Shaw believes in himself is very refreshing in these atheistic days when so many believe in no God at all."

 The British poet **Lascelles Abercrombie** had an equally original response when he was challenged to a duel by fellow poet **Ezra Pound.**

Knowing that Pound was talented with a sword, Abercrombie chose another weapon, responding, "May I suggest that we bombard each other with unsold copies of our own books?"

That duel, which many looked forward to, was never fought.

 Writer **Mark Twain:** "Shakespeare is dead and gone. Milton has been gathered unto his fathers. Tennyson is no longer with us, and, ladies and gentlemen, I am not feeling very well myself."

MY TURN
THE DOUBLE REMAKE

Always looking to make something new from something old, Hollywood screenwriters are creating Double Remakes, movies that combine two successful films into one profitable sequel.

Coming soon to a multiplex near you: *Rocky VII, Gandhi II.*

In this action-packed, spiritually uplifting Civil War boxing epic, the Mahatma may pray for peace but he packs a terrific left hook. Gandhi leads a protest march until he gets a shot at Rocky's title.

After defending his championship belt against bruisers like Apollo Creed, Mr. T, and Scary Russian Guy, Rocky is so punch-drunk that he converts to pacifism. Unfortunately for Rocky, he converts in the middle of the first round, and is knocked out by what Gandhi calls his "nonviolent roundhouse."

"I am not punching him," Gandhi explains after the fight. "I am merely putting my fists where he should have removed his face."

CHAPTER 17

DARWIN WAS WRONG

IS HISTORY JUST A JOKE?

"He had all the backbone of a chocolate éclair."

That was President **Theodore Roosevelt** putting President **William McKinley** in his place: squarely on the dessert table of history.

As recorded by the establishment, history is more usually the meat-and-potatoes pursuit of who controls the distribution of meat and who gets to hog the éclairs. But once you get out of school and pursue the oddities of history on your own, you can find quite a lot to laugh at, knowing that many of the great figures from the past would be laughing with you.

IT'S A FUNNY LIFE

 There were riots in the streets of Paris in 1830 as rival factions battled to control the throne of France.

When the master politician **Charles Talleyrand** heard the cathedral bells ringing in triumph, he announced, "We're winning."

"But who are 'we'?" a friend asked.

Talleyrand shrugged and said, "I'll tell you who we are tomorrow."

 Those to whom too much power is given tend to expect so much more. When King **Louis XIV** of France learned in 1704 that the British had defeated his army, he sent up a wail (since moaned by men with far lower expectations): "How could God do this to me, after all that I have done for Him?"

 King **Croesus** ruled the land of Lydia in the fifth century B.C. He contemplated war against Persia but was unsure that he could defeat such a mighty empire. So he asked the oracle of Delphi for guidance.

The oracle assured Croesus that if he went to war, he would destroy a great empire.

Fortified by the favorable prediction, the king ordered his army to attack the Persians, who then destroyed the Lydians in battle.

Feeling betrayed, Croesus demanded to know why the Delphic oracle had lied to him. The oracle insisted that she hadn't lied. Croesus had destroyed a great empire—his own.

 After President **John Quincy Adams** left the White House, he was elected to the House of Representatives, where he served until he died in his eighties.

When a much younger congressman criticized Adams for being too old to work in politics, Adams countered, "An ass is older at thirty than a man is at eighty."

 In the early days of the United States, delegates to the Constitutional Convention argued about how large an army the new nation could afford. One member introduced a motion to limit the standing army to five thousand men.

George Washington proposed an amendment to the motion that "no foreign army should invade the United States at any time with more than three thousand troops."

 During World War II, movie star **Merle Oberon** toured British hospitals to comfort wounded soldiers. When told that one soldier had killed a Nazi in hand-to-hand combat, Oberon asked, "With which hand?" Then the beautiful star kissed the GI's hand.

The soldier in the next bed sat up and told her, "I killed a Nazi too. Bit him to death."

When **Benjamin Disraeli** was prime minister of England, he was overwhelmed by the number of supplicants who pestered him for position and title. He turned down one applicant, but put a bright spin on the rejection.

"I cannot give you a baronetcy," Disraeli said. "But you can tell your friends I offered you one and you refused it. That is far better."

 Cato the Elder was one of ancient Rome's great leaders. When his allies suggested they should campaign to have a statue erected in his honor, Cato declined.

He explained, "I would rather have people ask, 'Why isn't there a statue to Cato?' than 'Why is there one?'"

 Benjamin Franklin defended the Constitution of the United States from the challenges of a dissatisfied opponent, who said, "Those words mean nothing. Where is all the happiness you say it guarantees us?"

"The Constitution only guarantees the American people the right to pursue happiness," Franklin responded. "You have to catch it yourself."

 After the frontiersman **Davy Crockett** served his Tennessee constituency in the nation's capital, he returned home and stopped at a backwoods store, where a crowd gathered to hear about life in the big city.

Crockett explained that people in Washington had a totally different way of telling time than normal folks. They rise to eat breakfast when the sun has been up long enough for you folks to have done half a day's work, he told them. They eat a meal they call lunch in the afternoon, then wait for dinner until it gets dark.

One backwoods hunter scratched his head and asked, "But when do they eat their supper, Davy?"

Crockett shook his head and said, "They're so busy in Washington, they don't even get to supper until the next day."

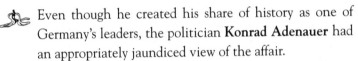 Even though he created his share of history as one of Germany's leaders, the politician **Konrad Adenauer** had an appropriately jaundiced view of the affair.

"History," he said wisely, "is the sum total of things that could have been avoided."

Keeping up with Adenauer in the skillful use of cynicism was the American writer **Ambrose Bierce**, who defined history as "an account, mostly false, of events, mostly unimportant, which are brought about by rulers, mostly knaves, and soldiers, mostly fools."

Franz Boas, a professor of anthropology at Columbia University, did not support America's entrance into World War I because he was more interested in understanding human nature than destroying it.

When the college administration asked the faculty to fill out a form indicating what they would do to support the war effort, Boas sent his back with a simple response: "Mind my own business."

FROM THE JOKE FILE

1. A history teacher told his class the story of **George Washington** chopping down his father's cherry tree, then admitting that he'd done it. "Do you know why George's father didn't punish him?" the teacher asked his students.

   One little boy raised his hand and guessed, "Because George still had the ax in his hand."

2. A Cheyenne from South Dakota took a trip to New York City. When he bought a hot dog at one of those street corner stands, the vendor asked him, "So how do you like our city?"

   "I like it fine," the Cheyenne said. "How do you like our country?"

WHAT THE PROS SAY

 Radio comedian **Stan Freberg:** "First, you hock the jewels, you give me the money, and I buy the ships. Then I discover the new world, you dump the king, and I'll send for you."

 Writer **Samuel Butler:** "God cannot alter the past, though historians can."

 Comic **Mort Sahl:** "There were four million people in the colonies, and we had Jefferson and Franklin. Now we have over 200 million, and the two top guys are Clinton and Dole. What can you draw from this? Darwin was wrong."

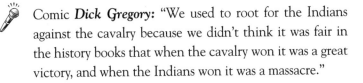

Comic **Dick Gregory:** "We used to root for the Indians against the cavalry because we didn't think it was fair in the history books that when the cavalry won it was a great victory, and when the Indians won it was a massacre."

Newspaper columnist **George Will:** "World War II was the last government program that really worked."

Writer **François Voltaire:** "The ancient Romans built their greatest masterpieces of architecture, their amphitheaters, for wild beasts to fight in."

Writer **Garrison Keillor:** "It was luxuries like air-conditioning that brought down the Roman Empire. With air-conditioning their windows were shut, they couldn't hear the barbarians coming."

Writer **François Voltaire:** "Neither holy, nor Roman, nor empire."

Writer **Havelock Ellis:** "What we call progress is the exchange of one nuisance for another nuisance."

Philosopher **Friedrich Nietzsche:** "Insanity in individuals is something rare. But in groups, parties, nations, and epochs it is the rule."

Comic **Steve Allen:** "What Voltaire actually said was this: 'I do not agree with what you say, sire, though I will defend to the death your right to say it. But for now, shut up!'"

Writer **Henry Becque:** "What makes equality such a difficult business is that we only want it with our superiors."

Cartoonist **Doug Larson:** "The reason people blame things on previous generations is that there's only one other choice."

Comic **Jerry Seinfeld:** "It's amazing that the amount of news that happens in the world every day always just exactly fits the newspaper."

Writer **E. B. White:** "There is nothing more likely to start disagreement among people or countries than an agreement."

Writer **George Bernard Shaw:** "Science is always wrong. It never solves a problem without creating ten more."

Writer **Don Marquis:** "The chief obstacle to the progress of the human race is the human race."

Comic **Emo Philips:** "Countries are making nuclear weapons like there's no tomorrow."

MY TURN
THE NEAR-GREAT KANN

It's hard to find a good horde these days. So the Near-Great Kann told me as the campfires sputtered through the night, and so I record on this scroll for all who follow.

With the Mighty Genghis dominating northern lands and the Great Khan Himself III plundering the wealthy estates of the south, pickings have been slim for the half-mongrel warriors of the Near-Great Kann, we who strike persistent annoyance in the hearts of all who have heard the onrushing clatter of our mules and felt the dull edge of our blades.

As camp historian and second cook, it falls to me to record the saga of our passing among the peoples we would surely have conquered if they had stood still longer, but whose daily routines we have most certainly disrupted.

In camp you hear the typical grumblings of second-rate hordes—the spoils are already spoiled before we get to them. But as the Kann says, if pike fodder had any sense, they would go into a different line of work, such as running for their lives.

"If anyone actually demanded a strict accounting," the Near-Great Kann admitted, "they would see that we're operating the horde at a significant deficit.

"The only way to keep a horde viable is to attack enemies who will wipe out a reasonable portion of my men, so that I don't have to feed and arm them. This is a self-canceling strategy.

"Furthermore, we have ridden across so many steppes that my lumbago is killing me. Hordes are a young man's game. That's why I've decided to settle down and raise a second family with a woman whose first husband ran away with a third-rate horde. Conquering is not what it used to be."

And so I assisted the Near-Great Kann to negotiate a truce with the village: He and his horde would not attempt to find enough fuel to put the village to the torch in exchange for the right of all horde members in good standing to turn their swords into plows and their mules into mules and become villagers themselves.

CHAPTER 18

THE MOST UNEXPECTED JOKE

AND OTHER THINGS TO LAUGH ABOUT AS YOU GET OLD

As you get older, laughing becomes optional. The advantage is that it gives you time off from all the crying opportunities life has to offer you.

Which raises an old question: How come bad TV shows have a laugh track, but not a cry track?

Now what were we talking about? Oh yeah, getting old. Or should it be getting olde? Either way, what's so funny about it, eh?

IT'S A FUNNY OLD LIFE

 Photographer **Ruth Van Bergen** specialized in celebrity portraits. One wealthy woman complained that Van

Bergen's photo wasn't nearly as good as the first one she had taken.

"You must forgive me," the photographer said diplomatically. "The last time I took your picture, I was ten years younger."

When West Germany's Chancellor **Konrad Adenauer** was ill, he asked his doctor to give him something so he could keep up the hectic pace of his work.

"I can't make you young again," the doctor cautioned.

"I don't want to become young again," Adenauer insisted. "All I want is to go on getting old."

When the ancient Roman **Cato** turned eighty, he began a new set of studies in Greek literature. A friend inquired why he would start a complex study at such an advanced age. Cato explained that it was the youngest age he had left.

A friend chided Senator **Chauncey Depew** for not getting enough exercise. Depew replied, "I get my exercise acting as pallbearer to my friends who exercise."

George Jessel was a standup comic with a thousand one-liners. One of his specialties was giving eulogies at the funerals of Hollywood celebrities.

Singer **Eddie Cantor** admired Jessel's talents at funerals, but thought his intentions a little odd. "All through the years he makes notes on his friends," Cantor observed. "He wants to be ready."

 When glamorous Hollywood actresses reach their forties, they usually run out of parts. But if they stay in the business into their sixties and beyond, different roles become available to them. Not all of the actresses think that's such a good thing.

When **Elsa Lanchester** started to age, she sneered, "I hope I never live so long that I get hired simply for not being a corpse."

 Jimmy Breslin, the crusading New York City newspaper columnist, had a unique way of dealing with the death of friends. When people he liked grew old and died, he crossed out their phone numbers in his address book and wrote above: 1-800-HEAVEN.

BONUS LAUGH
DYING IS EASY

 Writer **Sholom Aleichem:** "No matter how bad things get, you got to go on living, even if it kills you."

 Writer **Somerset Maugham:** "Death is a very dull, dreary affair, and my advice to you is to have nothing whatever to do with it."

☆ Comic **Moms Mabley:** "They say you shouldn't say nothing about the dead unless you can say something good. He's dead, *good!*"

☆ Comic **George Burns:** "I don't believe in dying. It's been done. I'm working on a new exit. Besides, I can't die now—I'm booked."

☆ Comic **Jerry Seinfeld:** "Living is good and dying . . . not as good."

☆ Comic **Steven Wright:** "I intend to live forever. So far, so good."

FROM THE JOKE FILE

1. Ed thought the new doctor looked familiar. Spotting the doctor's degree on the wall, he realized they'd both gone to UCLA. But they couldn't have gone there at the same time, Ed thought. This doctor was much older—bald, overweight, wrinkled.

   "When were you at UCLA?" Ed asked.

   "Early '70s," the doctor said.

   "That's amazing," Ed said. "I was there at the same time."

   "Really," the doctor said. "What did you teach?"

2. Inside every older person is a younger person wondering what the hell happened.

3. When his mother-in-law died, Ernie was asked by the funeral home director, "Shall we prepare for a cremation or a burial?" "Both," Ernie said. "Let's not take any chances."

WHAT THE PROS SAY

 Comic **George Burns:** "When I was young, I was called a rugged individualist. When I was in my fifties, I was considered eccentric. Here I am doing and saying the same things I did then and I'm labeled senile."

 Comic **Jerry Seinfeld:** "They live in those minimum-security prisons, that's where they put all the old people. What's with all the security there? . . . Are the old people trying to escape, or . . . are people stealing old people? What is the security problem?"

 Comic **Joan Rivers:** "You know you're getting old when work is a lot less fun and fun is a lot more work."

 Magazine columnist **Robert Benchley:** "As for me, except for an occasional heart attack, I feel as young as I ever did."

 Writer **Edna Ferber:** "Being an old maid is like death by drowning, a really delightful sensation after you cease to struggle."

Writer **J. B. Priestley:** "When I was young there was no respect for the young, and now that I am old there is no respect for the old. I missed out coming and going."

 Comic **Joan Rivers:** "There are three sure signs of getting old. The first is loss of memory. I forget the other two."

 Comic **George Burns:** "When I was a boy, the Dead Sea was only sick."

 Comic **Lucille Ball:** "The secret of staying young is to live honestly, eat slowly, and lie about your age."

 Comic **George Burns:** "If you live to be one hundred, you've got it made. Very few people die past that age."

 Nineteenth-century lecturer **Josh Billings:** "I have never known a person to live to be one hundred and be remarkable for anything else."

 Comic **George Burns:** "I'm very pleased to be here. Let's face it, at my age I'm very pleased to be anywhere."

 Writer **James Thurber:** "Old age is the most unexpected of all the things that can happen to a man."

 Writer **Peter Cook** (from a theatrical skit with partner **Dudley Moore**):

DUDLEY: So poor old Bender's dead.

PETER: Completely dead, yes.

DUDLEY: I'm so sorry. I had no idea.

PETER: Nor did Bender, really.

Writer **James Thurber:** "I'm sixty-five and I guess that puts me in with the geriatrics. But if there were fifteen months in every year, I'd only be forty-eight. That's the trouble with us. We number everything. Take women, for example. I think they deserve to have more than twelve years between the ages of twenty-eight and forty."

MY TURN
ENGLISH RE-LIT

One advantage of growing old is picking up your education where you left off when you were young by returning to the specially designed classes of senior colleges like Old and Hostile U.

There you can study such subjects as English Lit for People 101: Previously Unanalyzed Shakespearean Characters. Here's a sample of the coursework:

1. Lord Beaverbrook, chairman of King Lear's Estate Planning Commission, enters.

    "Sire, we feel a nice set of cookware is always a good gift for daughters. But if you insist upon dividing the kingdom, hang on to that summer castle—just in case it doesn't work out with the girls. You know how they're always squabbling over something."

2. Glorianna-Sue, the castle maid, follows Lady Macbeth into the courtyard.

"And, Lady, I just put fresh sheets on all the beds in the guest wing, so I hope, you know, there's not going to be such a mess like last time. Those damn spots, they don't come out in the wash."

CHAPTER 19

GOD MAKES THE GRADE

AND OTHER CURIOSITIES OF RELIGION

"Lord, if you can't make me a better boy," a little boy prayed, "don't worry about it. I'm having a real good time like I am."

God obviously has a great sense of humor. He made us.

IT'S A FUNNY AFTERLIFE

 The priest **Andrew Agnellus** consulted for British television when producers had questions about the authentic presentation of Catholic views in their shows.

One TV exec asked the priest how he could obtain the official Catholic view of heaven and hell.

Agnellus had a one-word answer: "Die."

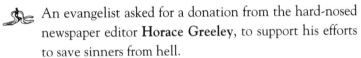 Yale professor **William Phelps** was grading papers on a tough test. One of his students gave a clever response to a particularly difficult philosophical problem: "God alone knows the answer to this question."

Phelps gave the test back to the student with this remark: "God gets an A. You get an F."

 An evangelist asked for a donation from the hard-nosed newspaper editor **Horace Greeley**, to support his efforts to save sinners from hell.

"I'll not give a damned cent," Greeley said. "Not half enough of them go there now."

 When someone asked Irish playwright **Brendan Behan** if he was Jewish, he responded, "I am not. But our Blessed Lord is. I hope I've caught a little of the contagion."

 Even when he was an old man, **Michelangelo** continued to work diligently at his art. A friend asked him with so much unfinished whether it was difficult to know his death could come at any moment.

No, Michelangelo said, he accepted death. "Since life was such a pleasure, death coming from the same great source cannot displease us."

Prior to a title match against **James Corbett**, a friend went to visit the heavyweight champ **Bob Fitzsimmons** and found the boxer's wife praying for her husband's victory.

"Won't you join her in prayer?" the friend asked.

"No, my wife is more devout than I am," Fitzsimmons said. "If He won't do it for her, He certainly won't do it for me."

FROM THE JOKE FILE

1. An atheist went out for a walk on Christmas Eve. As he turned down a dark street, he saw a bright red light in the sky. As the light grew bigger and brighter, he could see it was the nose of a flying reindeer, leading a sleigh of other flying reindeer through the air. Looming over the back of the sled was a giant fat man with a white beard in a red suit.

   But the fat man, the sleigh, and the reindeer were headed straight for him, about to land right on his head.

   "Dear God, help me," the man cried out.

   From the sky came the voice of God, "I thought you didn't believe in Me."

   "I know," the atheist shouted. "But until a minute ago, I didn't believe in Santa Claus, either."

2. A Russian professor and an American professor were arguing about the Bible. "Not only did we write the Bible," the Russian professor declared, "but Adam and Eve were Russian."

   "An absurd idea," the American professor replied.

   "Look at the evidence," the Russian professor argued. "They had nothing to wear, only an apple to eat, and their boss thought he was God. Despite all that, they claimed they were in paradise."

3. A minister was disappointed when he took up the collection from his congregation. "You know you can't take it with you," he told them. "But if you put it in the plate, I'll send it on ahead."

4. An eccentric was dying, and a priest urged him to make his peace with the world. "Denounce Satan," the priest begged him. "You must curse the devil with your last breath."

   The individualist shook his head and said nothing.

   "Why do you refuse to denounce the devil?" the priest asked.

   The man shrugged. "Until I know where I'm heading," he said, "I don't want to tick anyone off."

WHAT THE PROS SAY

 Writer **Woody Allen:** "If only God would give me some clear sign—like making a large deposit in my name at a Swiss bank."

 Comic **Bob Newhart:** "Growing up Catholic in Chicago, the best time to go to confession was during the Notre Dame–SMU game. You could tell that priest anything. 'I just killed my family.'

"'Well, don't do it again, my son,' and you could hear the game on in the background."

Writer **Woody Allen:** "If you want to make God laugh, tell him your future plans."

 Comic **Jeffrey Jena:** "I would rather know fifty gays than one Jehovah's Witness. You won't ever see a gay at your front door trying to convert you."

 Comic **Ronnie Shakes:** "Last month I blew five thousand dollars at a reincarnation seminar. I got to thinking: What the hell, you only live once."

 Writer **Douglas Adams:** "There is a theory which states that if ever anyone discovers exactly what the universe is for and why it is here, it will instantly disappear and be replaced by something even more bizarre and inexplicable. There is another theory which states that this has already happened."

 Writer **Woody Allen:** "Suffering is really God's will, although why He gets such a kick out of it is beyond me."

 Comic **Mort Sahl:** "Most people past college age are not atheists. It's too hard to be in society, for one thing, because you don't get any days off. And if you're an agnostic, you don't know whether you get them off or not."

 Poet **Dante Gabriel Rossetti:** "The worst moment for the atheist is when he is really thankful and has nobody to thank."

 Comic **Joan Rivers:** "When atheists just barely avoid accidents, do you think they say, 'Thank nobody'?"

Writer **G. K. Chesterton:** "Angels fly because they take themselves lightly."

 Philosopher **Friedrich Nietzsche:** "A casual stroll through the lunatic asylum shows that faith does not prove anything."

 Writer **François Voltaire:** "God is a comedian playing to an audience too afraid to laugh."

 Comic **Denis Leary:** "You know what hell is, folks? It's Andy Gibb singing 'Shadow Dancing' for eons and eons. And you have to wear orange plaid bell bottoms and sit next to the Bay City Rollers."

 Writer **Woody Allen:** "There is the fear that there is an afterlife, but no one will know where it's being held."

 Radio comic **Fred Allen:** "Most of us spend the first six days of each week sowing wild oats. Then we go to church on Sunday and pray for a crop failure."

 Comic **Ellen DeGeneres:** "In the beginning there was nothing. God said, 'Let there be light!' And there was light. There was still nothing, but you could see it a whole lot better."

 Comic **Bob Hope:** "I do benefits for all religions. I'd hate to blow the hereafter on a technicality."

 TV comic **Bill Maher:** "Suicide is man's way of telling God, 'You can't fire me. I quit.'"

Writer **Jane Wagner:** "When we talk to God, we're praying. When God talks to us, we're schizophrenic."

 Writer **H. L. Mencken:** "It is impossible to imagine the universe run by a wise, just, and omnipotent God. But it is quite easy to imagine it run by a board of gods."

 Writer **Quentin Crisp:** "I simply haven't the nerve to imagine a being, a force, a cause which keeps the planets revolving in their orbits and then suddenly stops in order to give me a bicycle with three speeds."

 Comic **Emo Philips:** "When I was a kid I used to pray every night for a new bicycle. Then I realized that the Lord doesn't work that way. So I stole one and asked Him to forgive me."

 Writer **Alexandre Dumas:** "If God were suddenly condemned to live the life which He has inflicted upon men, He would kill himself."

 Writer **Garrison Keillor:** "God writes a lot of comedy . . . The trouble is, He's stuck with so many bad actors who don't know how to play funny."

 Writer **H. L. Mencken:** "Imagine the Creator as a stand-up comedian, and at once the world becomes explicable."

 Writer **Malcolm Muggeridge:** "Every happening, great and small, is a parable whereby God speaks to us, and the art of life is to get the message."

Writer **Friedrich Nietzsche:** "In heaven all the interesting people are missing."

 Writer **Evelyn Waugh:** "It is a curious thing that every creed promises a paradise which will be absolutely uninhabitable for anyone of civilized taste."

 Writer **Aldous Huxley:** "Maybe this world is another planet's hell."

 Writer **Peter Cook:** "I say a little prayer. I say, 'Dear God in heaven, if You're there, heed my prayer. If You're not there, don't take any notice.'"

MY TURN
GOD OF THE TIGERS

You don't get into a good college without doing well on your SATs. Why should heaven have lower admission standards?

Maybe God will establish IQ tests for entry into heaven. Or does He really want to spend the rest of eternity with a bunch of idiots?

Those who fail to meet the admission requirements could take remedial classes as part of our national No Ex-person Left Behind program.

They'll have to answer the big question: If people are too stupid to live, will they be just as stupid in the afterlife?

And also the medium-size question: Will God be nice and make you smarter when you die, as well as better looking? Or can you flunk out of the afterlife too?

For bonus points, they can try the little question: Is that a left when you get to the end of the tunnel, or a right?

Then there's the essay test: In ten million words or less, explain why God didn't make a world full of lambs and goldfish.

It would have been such a lovely place, so peaceful. But He did not. You ever wonder why He made the sharks and tigers? Because it was no skin off His nose, that's why.

CHAPTER 20

NEVER PICK A FIGHT WITH AN UGLY PERSON

ODDS AND ENDS

"I think I've discovered the secret of life," Peanuts cartoonist **Charles Schulz** said. "You just hang around until you get used to it."

While you're hanging around, you can enjoy a few good laughs from my collection of comedy leftovers.

IT'S A FUNNY LIFE

 The writer **Isaac Bashevis Singer** came up with a clever if puzzling solution to the philosophical question: Do people have free will, or are our lives predestined?

"We have to believe in free will," Singer explained. "We've got no choice."

 Ad man **John Yeck** also ran the Let's Have Better Mottoes Association. Here are two of his best:

"People who live in stone houses shouldn't throw glasses."

"To get a job done well, give it to a busy man. His secretary will do it."

 The children's book writer **Dr. Seuss** made kids laugh and astounded them with his wildly imaginative stories. Then there was the young fan who astounded Dr. Seuss with this letter:

"Dear Dr. Seuss: You sure thunk up a lot of funny books. You sure thunk up a million funny animals. Who thunk you up, Dr. Seuss?"

 MGM boss **Samuel Goldwyn** identified one of the dilemmas of our modern age when he asked, "Why should people go out and pay money to see bad films when they can stay at home and see bad TV for nothing?"

 Yankee skipper **Casey Stengel** was talking about baseball, but his managerial approach would apply to any business. "The key to being a good manager," he explained, "is keeping the people who hate me away from those who are still undecided."

An astronomer told **Albert Einstein**, "To an astronomer, man is nothing more than an insignificant dot in an infinite universe."

"I have often felt that," Einstein agreed. "But then I realize that the insignificant dot who is man is also the astronomer."

 Yankee slugger **Yogi Berra** offered this bit of dugout wisdom: "In theory there is no difference between theory and practice. In practice there is."

 British prime minister **Winston Churchill** failed in politics almost as often as he succeeded. That experience of both sides gave him an eyes-open view of the relationship between government and truth.

"Men occasionally stumble over the truth," he said. "But most of them pick themselves up and hurry off as if nothing had happened."

 Scientist **Albert Einstein** was unfazed that his radical theory of relativity was initially rejected by most of the scientific establishment. In one publication, a hundred science professors offered arguments that Einstein was wrong. But the physicist was unperturbed by their opposition.

"If I had been wrong," Einstein countered, "one professor would have been enough."

 Tennis star **Jimmy Connors** understood the dilemma of learning lessons the hard way. "Experience is a great advantage," he said. "The problem is that when you get the experience, you're too damned old to do anything about it."

BONUS LAUGH
JUST FOOLING AROUND

Kings used to have their court jesters. Villages had their idiots. We haven't gotten rid of the fools; we just have a lot of unemployed jokers.

☆ Cartoonist **Scott Adams:** "If there are no stupid questions, then what kind of questions do stupid people ask? Do they get smart just in time to ask questions?"

☆ Writer **Douglas Adams:** "A common mistake that people make when trying to design something completely foolproof is to underestimate the ingenuity of complete fools."

☆ Writer **P. J. O'Rourke:** "I like to think of anything stupid I've done as a 'learning experience.' It makes me feel less stupid."

☆ Writer **James Thurber:** "You can fool too many of the people too much of the time."

☆ Comic **Will Rogers:** "There is nothing so stupid as the educated man if you get off the thing he was educated in."

Magazine columnist **Robert Benchley:** "Drinking makes such fools of people, and people are such fools to begin with, that it's compounding a felony."

 Nineteenth-century lecturer **Josh Billings:** "Take all the fools out of this world and there wouldn't be any fun living in it, or profit."

FROM THE JOKE FILE

1. A philosopher went into a bar and had a drink. When the bartender asked if he'd like another, the philosopher said, "I think not," and disappeared.

2. A Zen monk was challenged by an acolyte who took a bird from a cage and asked the monk if the bird was alive or dead. If the monk said the bird was alive, the student planned to wring its neck. If he said the bird was dead, the student would release it.

   "My friend," the monk said, "the matter is entirely in your hands."

3. "I take my hat off to my barber."
   "That good, is he?"
   "No, but it's the only way he can cut my hair."

4. My cousin's not too bright. She got an AM radio. Took her a month to figure out she could use it at night.

WHAT THE PROS SAY

 Comic **Robin Williams:** "Never pick a fight with an ugly person. They've got nothing to lose."

 Writer **Peter De Vries**: "The universe is like a safe to which there is a combination. But the combination is locked up in the safe."

 Writer **Garrison Keillor:** "Cats are intended to teach us that not everything in nature has a purpose."

 Writer **Woody Allen:** "Today I saw a red and yellow sunset and thought, How insignificant I am. Of course, I thought that yesterday too, and it rained."

 Writer **James Thurber:** "There is no safety in numbers or in anything else."

 Comic **Steven Wright:** "Plan to be spontaneous tomorrow."

 Cartoonist **Doug Larson:** "Wisdom is the quality that keeps you from getting into situations where you need it."

 Writer **Woody Allen:** "The lion and the calf shall lie down together, but the calf won't get much sleep."

 Writer **William Burroughs:** "Most of the trouble in this world has been caused by folks who can't mind their own business because they have no business of their own to mind, any more than a smallpox virus has."

Writer **Jane Wagner:** "You can't expect insights, even the big ones, to suddenly make you understand everything. But I figure, hey, it's a step if they leave you confused in a deeper way."

 Writer **Robert Benchley:** "Nothing is more responsible for the good old days than a bad memory."

 Cartoonist **Charles Schulz:** "No problem is so big or so complicated that it can't be run away from."

 Writer **Will Rogers:** "The best way to make a fire with two sticks is to make sure that one of them is a match."

 Comic **George Carlin:** "Whose cruel idea was it for the word *lisp* to have an *s* in it?"

 Comic **Dick Gregory:** "America will tolerate the taking of a human life without giving it a second thought. But don't misuse a household pet."

 Comic **Steven Wright:** "I'm living on a one-way, dead-end street. I don't know how I got there."

 Cartoonist **Doug Larson:** "For disappearing acts, it's hard to beat what happens to the eight hours supposedly left after eight of sleep and eight of work."

 Comic **Ellen DeGeneres:** "People always ask me, 'Were you funny as a child?' Well, no, I was an accountant."

Comic **Steven Wright:** "I have the world's largest collection of seashells. I keep it on all the beaches of the world. Perhaps you've seen it."

Comic **Paula Poundstone:** "The problem with cats is that they get the exact same look on their face whether they see a moth or an ax murderer."

Comic **Steven Wright:** "If toast always lands butter-side down, and cats always land on their feet, what happens if you strap toast on the back of a cat and drop it?"

Writer **James Thurber:** "No other thing in the world falls so far short of being able to do what it cannot do as a pigeon does. Or being unable to do what it can do, too, as far as that goes."

Comic **Spike Milligan:** "I can speak Esperanto like a native."

Writer **Douglas Adams:** "For a moment, nothing happened. Then after a second or so, nothing continued to happen."

Writer **Fran Lebowitz:** "To put it rather bluntly, I am not the type who wants to go back to the land. I am the type who wants to go back to the hotel."

Writer **Woody Allen:** "I took a speed-reading course and read *War and Peace* in twenty minutes. It's about Russia."

Writer **Raymond Chandler:** "Chess is as elaborate a waste of human intelligence as you can find outside an advertising agency."

 Comic **Steven Wright:** "I almost had a psychic girlfriend, but she left me before we met."

 Comic **Gracie Allen:** "Smartness runs in my family. When I went to school, I was so smart my teacher was in my class for five years."

 Comic **Steven Wright:** "When I woke up this morning, my girlfriend asked me, 'Did you sleep good?' I said, 'No, I made a few mistakes.'"

 Comic **Emo Philips:** "People come up to me and say, 'Emo, do people really come up to you?'"

 Writer **James Thurber:** "Well, if I called the wrong number, why did you answer the phone?"

 Comic **Steven Wright:** "I bought my brother some gift wrap for Christmas. I took it to the Gift Wrap Department and told them to wrap it, but in a different print so he would know when to stop unwrapping."

 Comic **Steven Wright:** "All those who believe in telekinesis, raise my hand."

 Movie comic **Groucho Marx:** "I have had a perfectly wonderful evening, but this wasn't it."

Writer **Raymond Chandler:** "From thirty feet away she looked like a lot of class. From ten feet away she looked like something made up to be seen from thirty feet away."

 Writer **Roger Price:** "We are educated only in the ways that a chimpanzee who sits at a table and drinks from a saucer is educated compared to a baboon."

 Comic **Groucho Marx:** "Next time I see you, remind me not to talk to you."

 Society wit **James McNeill Whistler:** "If other people are going to talk, conversation becomes impossible."

 Cartoonist **Charles Schulz:** "Don't worry about the world coming to an end today. It is already tomorrow in Australia."

MY TURN
WHAT IS LIFE ALL ABOUT, ANYWAY?

Maybe it's about nothing. If it was all about something, wouldn't someone have figured it out by now? Some idiot would have stumbled on the answer by accident, don't you think? The way they discovered vulcanized rubber or archaeology or the Backstreet Boys.

There are plenty of people who say they have figured it all out: Christians, Jews, seventeen Buddhists, ten million Republicans, two out of three college roommates, the Federal Commission to Figure Things Out.

They all keep a tight grip on the meaning of life. And the only people who disagree with them are everyone else.

We should hold a contest: Tell us why things are the way they are, in 250,000 words or more.

The winner gets to walk away with our grand prize: metaphysical certainty, guaranteed to last till your next bad mood or first drink, whichever you get to first.

Since we announced the contest in the paragraph above, we have already received two entries.

The first comes from the South Pacific, where a tribe of impossibly primitive people who couldn't create a really gnarled civilization if their lives depended on it, which in reverse they do, came up with the absurd belief that men were created from a branch of the sugar plant, while women were created from a different branch of the sugar plant.

This theory offers a comprehensive explanation of why men and women are different in some ways and not all that different in other ways, and also explains our sweet teeth: We're trying to go home again.

The second entry in the International Meaning of Life Contest comes from Dredward Wigglesworth, one of the Midwest's leading pre-existential philosophers and video store rewind clerks, and is called the Unified Field theory about how everything works. This theory can be summarized as: How the hell should I know? Where's the remote?

PART 2

THE COMEDY SLAMS

THE PROS FACE OFF IN A BATTLE OF WITS

Gunfighters used to get all the good showdowns. Now it's poets who stand up to each other in poetry slams.

Isn't it time for funny people to face off in the battle of wits?

THE MOVIE SLAM

Movie writers get paid big money for their clever lines, and a few of them actually earn it. Here are a few of the top guns in a Hollywood face-off:

☆ From *The Producers* (written by **Mel Brooks**): "He stinks. He's perhaps the worst director that ever lived. He's the only director whose plays close on the first day of rehearsal."

From *The Way We Were* (written by **Arthur Laurents**): "You really think you were easy? Compared to what—the Hundred Years War?"

From *Postcards from the Edge* (written by **Carrie Fisher**):

MERYL STREEP: Mom, I'm middle-aged.

SHIRLEY MACLAINE: *I'm* middle-aged.

STREEP: How many 120-year-old women do you know?

From *Bedazzled* (written by **Peter Cook**):

DUDLEY MOORE: You're a nutcake.

PETER COOK: They said the same of Jesus and Galileo . . .

MOORE: They said the same of a lot of nutcakes too.

From *Body Heat* (written by **Lawrence Kasdan**):

WILLIAM HURT: I need tending. I need someone to take care of me. Someone to rub my tired muscles, smooth out my sheets.

KATHLEEN TURNER: Get married.

HURT: I just need it for tonight.

 From *Four Weddings and a Funeral* (written by **Richard Curtis**): "I always just hoped that, that I'd meet some nice, friendly girl, like the look of her, hope the look of me didn't make her physically sick, then pop the question and, um, settle down and be happy. It worked for my parents. Well, apart from the divorce and all that."

JAY LENO
VS.
DAVID LETTERMAN

In this corner, the champ—an incredibly well-paid late-night TV talk show host. And in the other corner, the challenger—the other incredibly well-paid late-night TV talk show host.

Who's who? Well, one is funny and the other is . . . funny. One tells jokes based on events and people in the news, while the other tells jokes based on people and events in the news.

Okay, now that we've cleared that up, here they are, folks, let's give a big silent readers' welcome to Jay Leno and David Letterman.

Seven opening shots from TV comic **Jay Leno**:

1. "According to New York publishers, **Bill Clinton** will get more money for his book than **Hillary Clinton** got for hers. Well, duh. At least his book has some sex in it."

2. "[President] **Bush** said today he is being stalked. He said wherever he goes, people are following him. Finally, someone told him, 'Psst, that's the Secret Service.'"

3. "CNN found that **Hillary Clinton** is the most admired woman in America. Women admire her because she's strong and successful. Men admire her because she allows her husband to cheat and get away with it."

4. "I went into a McDonald's yesterday and said, 'I'd like some fries.' The girl at the counter said, 'Would you like some fries with that?'"

5. "Some Democrats say the estimated sixty-billion-dollar cost of a war with Iraq could be better spent at home. When he heard that, President **Bush** agreed and announced plans to bomb Ohio."

6. "The **Bush** administration said today there is a lot of support for us to attack Iraq. Exxon, Mobil, Texaco, Chevron—they're all lining up."

7. "The Pentagon still has not given a name to the Iraqi war. Somehow Operation Re-elect **Bush** doesn't seem to be popular."

TV comic **David Letterman** returns fire with seven shots of his own:

1. "Experts say that Iraq may have nuclear weapons. That's bad news. They may have a nuclear bomb. Now the good news is that they have to drop it with a camel."

2. "President **Bush** says he needs a month off to unwind. Unwind? When the hell does this guy wind?"

3. "New York now leads the world's great cities in the number of people around whom you shouldn't make a sudden move."

4. "We have defeated **Saddam Hussein** and Iraq. The good news is Iraq is ours, and the bad news is Iraq is ours."

5. "People say New Yorkers can't get along. Not true. I saw two New Yorkers, complete strangers, sharing a cab. One guy took the tires and the radio; the other guy took the engine."

6. "President **Bush** has been silent on **Schwarzenegger**. Of course, he can't pronounce *Schwarzenegger*."

7. "President **Bush** has said that he does not need approval from the U.N. to wage war, and I'm thinking: Well, hell, he didn't need the approval of the American voters to become president, either."

SNIPING OF THE RICH AND FAMOUS

Singer **Dean Martin:** "I once shook hands with **Pat Boone** and my whole right side sobered up."

British prime minister **Benjamin Disraeli** about British prime minister **William Gladstone:** "He is a man without a single redeeming defect."

Comic **Robin Williams:** "You'll notice that **Nancy Reagan** never drinks water when **Ronnie** speaks."

Movie star **Humphrey Bogart:** "The so-called **Rock Hudsons** and **Tab Hunters** are a dull bunch of cruds."

Movie star **Rock Hudson:** "I did not get **Lee Majors** his start in acting. You can't pin that one on me."

Movie star **Greer Garson** on **Marlon Brando:** "I do not enjoy actors who seek to commune with their armpits."

Writer **Truman Capote** on **Rod Steiger:** "He's the worst actor that ever lived. The very name makes me throw up."

Movie star **W. C. Fields** on **Charlie Chaplin:** "He's the best ballet dancer that ever lived, and if I get a good chance, I'll strangle him with my bare hands."

Movie star **Bette Davis** about **Marilyn Monroe:** "She's the original good time that was had by all."

Movie star **Tony Curtis** about costar **Marilyn Monroe:** "It was like kissing Hitler."

Actress **Hermione Gingold** on actress **Hermione Baddeley:** "It irritated me no end that we were often mistaken for sisters . . . I would tell interviewers, 'No, dear, she's the fat one.'"

Writer **Truman Capote:** "I am not a fan of **Meryl Streep**, or as I call her, Meryl Creep . . . Life is difficult enough without Meryl Streep movies."

Movie star **Arnold Schwarzenegger** on his wife, TV star **Maria Shriver:** "People are always making a fuss over my fifteen- to twenty-million-dollar salaries. Believe me, the amount is meaningless once my wife, Maria, finds out about it. She's already spent half of my salary from *Terminator 7*."

Movie director **Steven Spielberg** about movie director **George Lucas:** "He reminded me a little of **Walt Disney's** version of a mad scientist."

Writer **Mark Twain** about writer **Henry James:** "Once you've put one of his books down, you simply can't pick it up again."

Writer **T. S. Eliot** about **Henry James:** "He had a mind so fine that no idea could violate it."

Writer **Oscar Wilde:** "There are two ways of disliking poetry. One way is to dislike it, the other is to read **Pope.**"

Writer **Ralph Waldo Emerson: "Napoleon III** acquired such skill in the art of lying that you could not even depend upon the exact contrary of what he said."

Comic **Robin Williams** about pop star **Michael Jackson:** "He's like *Lord of the Rings*, the entire cast. Michael's about to jump species."

Comic **John Parrott: "Joan Collins** unfortunately can't be with us tonight. She's busy attending the birth of her next husband."

Movie star **David Niven** about movie star **Errol Flynn:** "You could always depend on Errol. He always let you down."

Actor **John Gielgud** about actress **Ingrid Bergman:** "She can speak five languages and can't act in any of them."

 Movie director **Sydney Pollack** about directing **Dustin Hoffman** in *Tootsie:* "I'd give [the Oscar nomination] up if I could have back the nine months of my life I spent with Dustin making it."

THE OPTIMISTS
VS.
THE PESSIMISTS

We all know pessimists are funny because they say the things that society's politicians and advertising execs don't want to admit are true. But can you be funny and optimistic at the same time? Have you ever met a funny optimist?

 Newspaper columnist **Earl Wilson:** "An optimist is someone who hasn't gotten around to reading the morning papers."

 Writer **Don Marquis:** "A pessimist is a person who has had to listen to too many optimists."

 Comic **Ronnie Shakes:** "I was going to buy a copy of *The Power of Positive Thinking,* and then I thought: What the hell good would that do?"

Writer **Oscar Wilde:** "Some cause happiness wherever they go; others, whenever they go."

Comic **Steven Wright:** "The light at the end of the tunnel has been turned off due to budget cuts."

Movie comic **W. C. Fields:** "Start every day with a smile and get it over with."

Playwright **Jean Kerr:** "Hope is the feeling that the feeling you have isn't permanent."

Writer **E. B. White:** "Man's curiosity, his relentlessness, his inventiveness, his ingenuity have led him into deep trouble. We can only hope that these same traits will enable him to claw his way out."

Comic **Flip Wilson:** "The cost of living's going up, and the chance of living's going down."

Writer **Raymond Chandler:** "It is not a fragrant world."

Cartoonist **Charles Schulz:** "I have a new philosophy. I'm only going to dread one day at a time."

Movie comic **W. C. Fields:** "A man's got to believe in something. I believe I'll have another drink."

Newspaper columnist **Marilyn vos Savant:** "At first, I only laughed at myself. Then I noticed that life itself is amusing. I've been in a generally good mood ever since."

Writer **Jonathan Swift:** "Blessed is he who expects nothing, for he shall never be disappointed."

 Writer **Bertolt Brecht:** "He who laughs last has not yet heard the bad news."

 Writer **E. B. White:** "Hang on to your hat. Hang on to your hope. And wind the clock for tomorrow is another day."

 Newspaper columnist **Franklin Pierce Adams:** "Every time we tell anybody to cheer up, things might be worse, we run away for fear we might be asked to specify how."

 Playwright **Jean Kerr:** "If you can keep your head when all about you are losing theirs, it's just possible you haven't grasped the situation."

THE CITY SLAM
THE COMEDIANS TAKE ON ONE OF THEIR FAVORITE TARGETS: NEW YORK CITY

 Comic **Denis Leary:** "New York teaches you to live life the way it should be lived—moment to moment, because every moment in New York could be your last."

TV comic **Johnny Carson:** "Anytime four New Yorkers get into a cab together without arguing, a bank robbery has just taken place."

 TV comic **David Letterman:** "Traffic signals in New York are just rough guidelines."

 Movie comic **Groucho Marx:** "Practically everybody in New York has half a mind to write a book, and does."

 Comic **Bob Newhart:** "A lion got loose in the Central Park Zoo, and was severely mauled."

 Comic **Will Rogers:** "I see where another wife out on Long Island shot her husband. Season opened a month earlier this year."

 TV comic **David Letterman:** "New York—when civilization falls apart, remember, we were way ahead of you."

 Comic **Anita Wise:** "I had to move to New York for health reasons. I'm extremely paranoid, and New York is the only place my fears are justified."

PART 3

COMEDY FROM
THE EVERYDAY LOUNGE

★ ★ ★ ★ ★ ★ ★ ★ ★

Why should professional comedians have all the fun? What if there was a club, the Everyday Lounge, where the performers were ordinary people who find comedy in real life?

Come on in. We've been holding a ringside table just for you.

Good evening, ladies and gentlemen, and the rest of you too. Tonight the Everyday Lounge is proud to present Ed Smedly, the world's funniest middle manager.

Hi folks, just flew in from a management seminar, and boy is the flight attendant tired. But that's the union's problem. Maybe you've been to this seminar. It's called "Beyond Multitasking:

242

The 17.5 Business Secrets of Highly Effective People Who Are Too Busy to Pass Them On to You for Anything Less Than $789.50."

What did they teach me about management? You get more work out of people if you treat them great and pay them really well.

But seriously, folks, the real secret of running a big business is to make them think if they don't work harder, they're going to lose their jobs. Because they are. We're going to outsource America, all of it.

The bad news: There's someone in India willing to work twice as hard as you for half the salary. The good news: There's another guy in China willing to work twice as hard as the guy in India, and he'll do it for nothing if his government tells him to. That's the one thing the communists are good at—labor management. No overtime in China, no strikes, no nothing.

But as we say in HR, ambiguity motivates. The paradox is not just a nonprofit Zen amusement any more. It's a productivity tool. Like everything else in the corporate world, the true test is not whether you're right but whether people think you're right.

It's like my boss always says, "It's not whether you win or lose that counts. It's whether I win or lose."

You have to go with your strengths. And if you don't have any strengths, then maybe that is your strength. So before I get back to work, folks, I want you to remember one thing: To err is human. To err over and over again is middle management.

People always ask us, where are the new comics coming from? And we tell them: Upper Loweria, in between Estonia and Justsaynoia. We found our next comic driving a taxi in Lower Manhattan. We knew he was a little off because he was driving a Boston cab. In his own country, he was known as the Upper Lowerian Carl Lewis. But we'll let him tell you that story himself. Please give an all-American welcome to Olympic star and funnyman Shleswig Undholstein.

How glorious it was to be the first athlete from the proud nation of Upper Loweria to participate in the Olympic Games, to take our place among the athletes of the world and raise the proud cry of our people: "We're number 187. We're number 187—maybe!"

Surely, in time, people will forget the minor commotion during the opening ceremonies. But as my country's sole representative, how did they expect me to carry our nation's flag and still wave to the crowd in a display of international waving?

I did drop the flagpole on a boxer from the nation of Luzerland. But I don't think I hit him hard enough to knock him down—even though he wouldn't get up again until we counted to ten.

Helping me pick up the pole, a synchronized swimming soloist from the nation of Miscellania said mine was the most unusual flag she'd seen in the parade.

I explained that my country didn't actually have a flag until my aunt Betsaweena said I could use her spare tablecloth. The flag's gray on a field of white depiction of my nation was not an official symbol of Upper Loweria but a stewed-millet stain.

As my country's sole Olympic athlete, I had been entered in every event, under the theory that Upper Loweria might set some kind of record if I came in last in all of them.

The Olympics' first event, gymnastics, went well until I showed up at the meet and saw what they expected me to do.

There is little in the training of a millet farmer to prepare you to risk your manhood on the pommel horse. But the doctors were kind to me afterward, considering that the only health care plan our nation has is a box of Band-Aids.

I figured I would do better at the marathon because I have actually run twenty-six miles in my life. Unfortunately, as the race started, I learned that they expected me to run all twenty-six miles on the same day.

By the time I finished the first half of the marathon, the race officials had moved on to other events.

I returned to my room in the Olympic Village, which I had been sharing with the field hockey team from the island nation of Tobe Namedlater. There I found that a TV crew assigned to film the activities of the other TV crews had moved in while I was out.

The swim competition went well, with me coming in as high as ninth in some of the eight-man heats.

At the medal ceremonies, which we watched from the back of the room on a portable TV set, a swimmer from East Westphailure told me I had broken new ground by being the first Olympic swimmer to race wearing water wings.

A full day of fencing, archery, handball, and cribbage proved a challenge. Although I did come in last in each of these events,

I did not embarrass my proud nation before the eyes of the world since there was nobody watching these events.

After coming in dead last in every event where I could actually locate the arena, I suppose what happened on the final day of the track-and-field competitions should not have surprised me.

I've been told it will make the highlight reels of every sports show until the next Olympics. Too bad no one in Upper Loweria saw what happened. While we do have cable in our proud country, we do not yet have any TV sets to which we can attach the cable.

The rules clearly state that a competitor in the pole vault can pass at the lower jumps and save his effort for the gold medal round. And that is what I did. Since I had never pole-vaulted before, I felt I might as well save it for one go at twenty-five feet than lose it all at eleven feet.

As I watched the other jumpers in their preliminary attempts, it became clear to me that the successful vaulters had an inner motivation that the failures lacked. So when it finally came my turn, I told the officials to raise the bar to world record height. I would no longer go for the zinc but for the gold.

I found out later that none of the officials spoke Lowerian. They thought I was there to pick up the pole towels of the top vaulters or they never would have let me on the track.

But as I sprinted down the runway, I thought: If I could only make this one jump, I would never have to compete in any more events, ever. That proved the ultimate motivation.

I thought, as I soared to victory, that all my problems were over. But there was one further embarrassment awaiting me.

As I mounted the podium to have the gold medal placed around my neck, an Olympic official whispered that the Olympic band needed the sheet music for the national anthem of Upper Loweria.

I was humiliated to explain that we had never written a national anthem, that a country whose motto is "We're number 187, we think" doesn't have that much to sing about.

"Just use that one you've been playing all week," I said. "But at the end, sub in 'Home of the millet farmer, land of the free refill.'"

And now a favorite here and in the classroom, it's high school history teacher Milbert Rhumes.

Okay, quiet down, everybody. Pop quiz: When you think of the really funny empires of history, who do you think of first?

Did everyone write down on their cocktail napkins that old favorite, the Roman Empire? The laugh riot of the B.C. world. Here's an ancient scroll I've been translating that records an encounter between the Roman gladiator Moviolus and the assistant manager of the Colosseum, Executorium.

So Executorium says: "Hail, big guy. At yesterday's matinee, what did you do?"

And Moviolus answers, "Fought ten men firing flaming arrows from chariots drawn by angry bears."

"Yes, and?"

"And I slew them."

"And the day before that?"

Moviolus thinks back. He's not real big on the whole remembering thing. So many sacrificial victims, so little time. Oh yeah. "I fought a dozen guys running with scissors while riding mildly depressed oxen."

"And you slew them?" Executorium asks.

"It's what I do."

"That's the problem, kid. Act's getting stale. Gate's down and the crowds are starting to drift over to the Christians."

"What do the Christians fight with?" Moviolus asks.

"They pray."

"That's it, prayer?"

"It's a novelty act," Executorium admits.

"Well, I pray, too."

"You do? When?"

"Whenever I'm attacked by ten men with flaming swords."

That gives Executorium an idea. "I'm thinking a little music," he says, "a few laughs, a big dance number, might liven up the show."

"I can't sing," Moviolus says. "And my contract calls for slaying, not dancing."

"That's why I'm bringing in a Greek chorus line," Executorium says.

"All right, but when they're done singing I get to kill them, right?"

"If they don't draw the crowd back, kid, I'll help you."

On our stage tonight, bringing his unique comic stylings to an exami-nation of the nature of existence, is the Right Round Reverend Medium Richard of the Church of the Persistent Second Thought.

So what's up with God? I mean, if we were created in His image, He might want to look into a little something called quality con-trol. We've got Nicole Kidman. Good move, God. But then we've also got Danny DeVito. They can't both be from the same image. That would be one weird-looking Omnipotence.

God must have a terrific sense of humor. After all, He invented us. I figure God majored in communications, minored in Thou Shalt Nots. Might have done us more good if He'd majored in biology, gotten the migraines and toothaches straightened out. Maybe other gods created their worlds in five days. Took ours seven.

Maybe He slept through some of the grunt classes like Intermediate Earthquakes, Volcanoes, and Floods—Should You Spare the Natural Disaster and Spoil the Race?

Then His professor asks, "How's that little green earth experiment of yours coming along?"

"I'm supposed to help those who help themselves, but you've never seen people who need so much help," God says. "Night after night. Never should have taught them that trick about praying. It never stops. I meant, like if you're really in big trouble. Not if you want a new bike."

"What seems to be the problem?" the professor asks.

"I told them, thou shalt not kill. Thought I was pretty straightforward on that one. But they've been killing each other ever since, just like I never said it."

"Perhaps they thought you meant thou shalt not kill *everyone*, but a certain percentage was okay," the professor reasons. "They don't kill everyone, do they?"

God has to admit, "They manage to keep it down to a hundred million or so a century."

"Taking Sundays off?"

"No, they pretty much work around the clock."

And the professor goes, "At least you have to admire their productivity."

"But I don't think they're following the spirit of the law," God complains.

One of the other gods, a real smug, all-powerful type, puts in his two cents. "It's all in how you write the commandments," he says. "I told my people no loud music after twelve."

"That's a good one," the professor says. "So you can get a little peace and quiet."

Now the guy's got to admit, "That's what I thought. They shut off the music at twelve, but then they just lie there and moan for the next eight hours. I should have been more specific."

All the other god students agree. "People, what can you do with them?"

"You can give them free will," our God says, "but you can't give them good taste."

Then the professor asks, "Anybody try a new approach?"

"I have," one of the A students says. "I gave mine no commandments at all."

"But that's anarchy," says one of the nervous gods, a real nerdy type. "Don't your people live in total chaos?"

"Yeah, just like yours. The only difference is mine never feel guilty about it. Cuts down on the whining by 80 percent."

Our next performer would be a great stand-up comedian if he didn't keep falling down. But that's his job. Or it would be if he had a job. Welcome Ratman Flynn, the funniest surfer in Malibu.

Dudes, what's up with waves?

All the surfers in southern Cal are bummed because the waves have flattened out big time, and I know why. Old surfers wore them down.

Too many big boards polished the tops right off the waves, just like sandpaper. I feel sorry for the kids coming up. They'll never know the thrill of having a 'mongous wave knock out your teeth with your toes.

And it's not just the old surfers ruining the waves, man. It's the whales, those rats. They flatten down the crests. Dude, the whales got too fat, eating all that high-calorie garbage the Love Boats dump over the side that the fat people won't eat. Fat whales, they're the worst.

Save the whales? No way, dude. What about our rides? That's what's wrong with the world—just when you think we've ruined everything that can be ruined, you realize we've only just begun.

Direct from her popular engagement with the Berkeley city council, it's vice mayor Emily Poston, the only politician who won't raise your taxes if you laugh at her.

We do things a little differently in Bezerkeley. At city council meetings, all residents are entitled to a turn at the open mike to make any kind of crazy proposal they want. We're into that whole free country routine, so there's no requirement that the proposal make any sense at all.

Last meeting one of the town's conservative feminists took the microphone and introduced a bill to require restaurants to have Meat and Non-meat sections. "It's not fair to vegetarians to make them inhale secondhand meat fumes," she argued.

A group of semi-enlightened birthed-again mothers from Free the Butterflies Middle School wanted us to "re-paradigm" the high school athletic programs.

"All sports should be noncompetitive," they said. "If a football team scores a touchdown, then the other team must be allowed to score an equal touchdown so the players don't go off the field feeling bad about themselves. All this winning and losing creates more losers than winners. We feel it's okay to lose as long as you learn to be more positive about the experience."

Finally, a neo-reactionary progressive wanted us to eliminate the city's traffic problems with alternate-day driving. If your license plate ends in an odd number, you drive on odd days only; even numbers on even days only.

"What about people with vanity plates?" a council member asked him.

"They get to drive only on Saturday night," he said, "the vanity night."

And that's Berkeley for you. You may think we're just a bunch of loony left-coasters, but consider this: Absurdity moves from left to right. Our culture is headed your way. You may laugh at us today, but you'll be laughing with us tomorrow. Good night, everyone, you've been swell.

PART 4

FREE LAUGHS

★ ★ ★ ★ ★ ★

We had plans to stop the book right here.

Well actually, back up there, right before we told you about our plans.

Then we thought: What about the laughless, the laugh-deprived, and the hard of laughing? Who's taking care of them? Obviously, not television.

Not to mention the people who want a higher rate of return on their comedy investments. And the people who will laugh at anything—they're our favorites.

So as a bonus for the laugh-positive among you, here is an extra section of Free Laughs. Now you can keep laughing for several more pages at no extra charge.

If you should find yourself not laughing, you're still ahead of the game financially since it hasn't cost you a thing. Either way, you're bound to get the last laugh.

OB-LA-DI, OB-LA-DADA

THE BEATLES' ANNOTATED HIT PARADE

Everyone knows that when the Beatles sang, "All together now," what they really meant was "All together in a little while from now."

The full message didn't scan properly, and John insisted on the compromise under the Music Before Meaning clause in their contract.

Footnote fans have been asking for the Top 13 less well-known annotations to the Beatles' legacy. So put on your dancing shoes, boys and girls, because the annotations to the hits are coming at you right now:

1. When the Beatles sang, "She loves me, yeah, yeah, yeah," and again "Love, love me do," and "If you saw my love, you'd love her too," not to mention "I've been in love before, and I found that love was more than just

holding hands," and even "All my loving, I will send to you," while not forgetting the unforgettable "You don't realize how much I need you, love you all the time and never leave you" (although some prefer "Say the word I'm thinking of, have you heard the word is love," while Beatle purists adhere to "In my life I love you more"), what they were really saying was "I like you a lot, perhaps more than a lot, a very large lot. But let's see how things work out because the song only lasts another forty-eight seconds and after that I may have to love someone else."

2. Consider this line: "But tomorrow may rain, so I'll follow the sun." Then also: "I'm in love, and it's a sunny day. Good day sunshine." Furthermore, "The sun is up, the sky is blue. It's beautiful and so are you."

   Here we clearly have the Beatles' early attempts to develop weather forecasting as an alternative career in case the music thing didn't work out.

3. The song "Here Comes the Sun" was not a philosophical defense of Galileo's contention that the sun was the center of the solar system, as many Beatle revisionists maintain. Nor was it a political statement in favor of solar energy, as has been advanced by the Beatles Division of the Friends of the Sun Society.

   Clearly, the song was written as an ironic comment on the Boys' own childhood growing up in the overcast of Liverpool and never knowing there was a sun until they were fourteen, or fourteen and a half in Ringo's case.

The line "And I say it's all right" was originally written as "And I say it's too bright." The change was made for the American market when the Fab Four's research team of Stills, Nash, Young, and Springsteen discovered that Americans were "sun sensitive" and were unlikely to buy records that insulted their favorite solar commodity.

4. "Dr. Robert" was, of course, Bob Dylan. But to demonstrate the depth of the Boys' songwriting talents, Dr. Robert was symbolically also Bobby Darin, Robert Redford, Robert De Niro, Bobby Dee and the Starlighters, Roberta Flack, and Dr. Bobby Roberts, the Beatles' official band podiatrist at the time.

Lesser-known historical figures in Beatle lore include Marlon Brando as Father McKenzie, Marilyn Monroe as Lovely Rita Meter Maid (displaying the Beatles' depth of biographical knowledge, as Monroe had listed "parking police" on her employment form as second choice to "movie idol"), Russ Wall (founder of Wall Drugs) as the Walrus, and Dwight D. Eisenhower (with whom the Boys had a short but intense correspondence when they were in their autograph-swapping phase) as both the Blue Meanie and the Fool on the Hill.

Noticeably absent from their litany of obscure personal references were Shakespeare and Attila the Hun. Most historians now agree that the Beatles saw Shakespeare as competition and didn't want to "put money in his pocket," as the English say.

But the curious absence of Attila in their music remains a symbolic mystery that divides historians. The Ringoists claim to have solved the mystery with the discovery of this note found among Ringo Starr's To Do lists:

"Note to Self: Hi, self! Tell John not to forget the Hun. Entire kingdoms made that mistake and regretted it. Why not 'Attila Vanilla in the Sky with Clubs' as a kind of country-rock-mazurka follow-up to Lucy?"

The Lucy of this note, however, was not the Lucy of the *Peanuts* comic strip, as early Beatles scholars mistakenly maintained for four or five months in 1983, but in actuality Peppermint Patty of the *Peanuts* strip in clever disguise.

In any event, the Anti-Ringoists claim that George was the actual author of Ringo's To Do lists because "As everyone in the music industry knows, a drummer has nothing to do."

5. *Rubber Soul*

The Beatles intended for the entire album to make no sense at all and see if they could get away with it. So far, so good.

6. The mystery song "78 1/2 Steps" is the secret song on the White album. Few people have actually heard it because records at that time didn't have secret songs.

    Still, the oft-neglected ballad does contain one line that is essential to an understanding of the driving force that drove the Boys at that time: "If I have to climb these damn steps one more time, I'm going back to Flattsbergh, yeah, yeah, yeah."

    The few fans who have figured out how to hear a song that doesn't exist know that it recounts the time George rented a fourth-floor flat on Penny Lane, then moved out two days later when he realized he would have to climb the stairs every time he went home. George was known as the Beatle most likely to go home in those giddy early days.

    Oddly enough, the same flat was later rented by Elton John, where he was inspired to write his first big hit, "What Do You Mean You Won't Install an Elevator, You Git?"

7. "Lady Madonna"

    The title is a misprint that the Fab Four let stand after deciding that if they got the printer mad at them they would only be inviting more typos and bigger labor disputes in the future.

    The song was originally about the time the Fab Two of Four went to the racetrack with John's dental hygienist girlfriend, Nora Wegian, and her American friend Donna (last name uncertain), who was in England doing graduate studies on the early symbolism in the work of Herman's Hermits.

Paul decided to bet one-pound-four on a horse named Late E for his nasty habit of starting the race only after the other horses had left the gate.

Paul and John wrote a song about the occasion, originally entitled "Late E, My Donna," a lyrical response to the American's question, "What stupid horse did you bet on this time, Paul?"

The exact nature of the relationship between Paul and Donna has been the subject of some debate among Beatles scholars at Cambridge over the past two decades.

Donna Nusbaum, a CPA from Passaic, New Jersey, emerged in 1987 to claim she was the original Donna and the song was written in retaliation because she refused to pay for her share of the fish and chips they had consumed during the races, maintaining that as a guest she should not have been expected to pony up.

The line "Wonder how you manage to feed the rest?" is a gamblers' lament that the Boys shared after losing all their bets at the track that day, reflecting their feelings about having to fall back upon their remaining $14.5 billion.

8. "Why," the Beatles sang, "don't we do it in the road?"

While many researchers have focused on exactly what they wanted to do in the road, our studies have led us to consider which road they wanted to do it in.

Certainly not Abbey Road, which had been so overrun by Beatles' collectors by this time that if they did do it in that road everyone would be watching.

We think they meant either Long or Winding Road. The latter, being more remote and having significant curves, would afford more opportunity to do whatever it was they wanted to do in the middle of it with no one watching.

9. In "Can't Buy Me Love" the Beatles sang, "I may not have a lot to give, but what I've got I'll give to you," thus instigating a legal brouhaha that has not abated to this day.

   Fans have repeatedly misinterpreted this remark as a legally binding contract and have over the decades approached various Beatles demanding all they have to give and seeming rather affronted when it is not given to them.

10. Perhaps the most notorious Beatles debate, mathematically speaking, surrounds Paul's contention that "Suddenly, I'm not half the man I used to be."

    Math scholars have long debated: If not 50 percent, then exactly how much of a man is Paul now compared to what he used to be?

Math conservatives continue to maintain that Current Paul is precisely 37 percent of Original Paul. Recent investigators into quantum physics contend that Paul has become a black hole of music and so is now an alternative reality of the man he used to be.

11. Further controversy shrouds the Beatles' claim that "Nothing is real and nothing to get hung about. Strawberry Fields forever."

Court authorities consider this a rather odd legal opinion since in England at the time there were many things one could get hung about.

Perhaps "Strawberry Fields" demonstrates why none of the Beatles ever became a lawyer, although several of them were known to watch *Rumpole of the Bailey* on the tube.

12. "We all live in a yellow submarine."

This is certainly the most revealing of all the Beatles' lines, in which the Fab Four demonstrate their amazing powers of prognostication.

When you read between the lines, you can see they predicted the rise of the Internet, the waffling of the stock market, the discovery of snowboarding, and the eventual World Series victory by the previously hapless Boston Red Sox.

Their prediction that giant marshmallows would be used to power cars of the future has not yet come to pass, although Beatles-loving scientists are working on the so-called Stay-Puft technology in the mountain labs of Colorado at this writing.

13. "I Want to Hold Your Hand"

Oddly enough, considering their later prolific output, the Boys struggled with this song through their early years in Germany, trying to nail down the lyrics before they dared a return to Britain.

Paul held out for "I want to hold your foot," while George favored "I want to hold your umbrella." John insisted that if they sang, "I want to hold your band," people would think they were being terribly clever and obscure, and this would be good for sales of the single as long as they put "Luv, Pass Me a Doughnut" on the flip side.

The band finally compromised on "hold your hand" only when Ringo's barber's girlfriend, whose name was either Ellen or Rigby (nobody is quite sure at this late date), shouted out, "Help! I've had a hard day's night listening to you idiots argue about this for the last eight days this week. Why don't you give up this terrible songwriting racket and go back to playing weddings?"

3 A.M. STRAY THOUGHTS

★ ★ ★ ★ ★ ★ ★ ★ ★

At 3 A.M. everything seems funny. Or nothing does.

In the middle of the night, writers entertain those stray thoughts that most people miss because they're asleep.

So in case you missed them, here are some of the stray thoughts you might have had at 3 A.M. if you'd been awake with a notebook and I'd stayed asleep.

WHO SLEPT WHERE?

We stayed at one of those quaint New England inns. Had a small plaque over the bed: "George Washington slept here."

I figured that's why the bed was so lumpy. They haven't changed the mattress since Washington slept on it. I only hope they've changed the sheets.

Ever since, I go around with my own set of plaques and nail them wherever I sleep. This may seem presumptuous, but I'm trying to be thoughtful. After I become president, I'll have saved plenty of Motel 6 owners a lot of trouble.

BUILDING A BETTER TOMORROW BY ACCIDENT

In America we're building a better tomorrow today—or by next Tuesday at the latest.

For many drivers, getting into a collision is not a happy experience, even though it's a way of meeting your neighbors.

But you don't have to let an accident ruin your day. After all, it's not what happens to you—it's how you look at it. You don't have to let a smashup put a dent in your attitude. Try to look on the bright side of personal disasters: We're all serving a useful purpose as crash-test dummies.

So have an accident today. It's not just a terrible waste of life. It's R&D. You can help to build a safer world by getting mangled, bent, compacted, defenestrated, or at least dinged up today.

ALMOST MAN OF THE YEAR

Did you hear that the Procrastination Society almost gave out its Man of the Year Award? The winner didn't show up at the banquet to claim his prize.

They would have been disappointed, getting stood up, but the award committee forgot which night they were holding the event, which no one noticed since the audience was a day late getting there.

COMPUTER DATING

Psychologists tell us that loneliness is a major cause of depression among singles. Actually, as any single can tell you, it's the other available singles out there who are the major cause of depression.

Finding people who share a common interest with you is hard when your only interest is how you can get away from all those jerks out there who think you share their only interest—themselves.

If you're looking for true romance, computer dating services are a great way to find exciting dates. For example, we found August 12, 1991, and February 3, 1983.

Computers eliminate the guesswork for the dating sensitive. After you've found a satisfactory date, you may try actually going out with a member of the opposite or similar sex—although you then face the modern dating dilemma: Who should pay on the first date?

Years ago, the man paid, under the theory that men could be talked into anything. Now it's a toss-up. How to decide?

As a general rule for anyone under the rank of general, the less good-looking of the two of you should pay. After all, the better looking can probably get another date. This could easily be your last.

KBAD RADIO, "ALL BAD, ALL THE TIME"

We'll be back in a minute with more bad music. But first, the bad news—which isn't that tough to find, folks. The air stinks. Traffic stinks. Work stinks. Can't afford a place to live. Food costs too much. Stinks too.

Yes, my friends, welcome to the twenty-first century—just like the twentieth century, only worse.

So come on over to KBAD and tune out those happy morning DJs. They're just trying to sell you junk. Remember, if the world didn't stink, they wouldn't have to spend so much time telling you how great everything is. If everything was great, you'd already know it.

We'll be back in a minute with the bad weather report. But first, a word from our bad sponsor.

Folks, as you lie there in utter despair wondering why you should ever get up again, don't you wish you could get your carpets a little cleaner?

That's why you need a Hopeless Vacuum Cleaner, from the only people who won't rip you off more than anyone else. That's Hopeless Vacuums. We know we suck. We're supposed to.

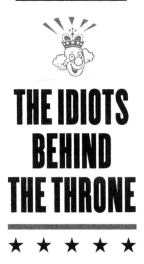

THE IDIOTS BEHIND THE THRONE

★ ★ ★ ★ ★

No power-mad king, dictator, or president ruins everything all by himself.

There's always some power-mad, shadowy figure whispering bright ideas in his ear, saying, "If only Caesar had listened to me, he would have stayed out of the salad business. It's like I told him, 'Beware the hives of March.' You don't want to go around scratching for the rest of your life. But did he listen to me? Noooo, and look where it got him."

BIG OX, CHIEF ADVISER

Look, Chief, if we wipe out Columbus and his men, the rest of those Euro-peons will come here to find out what happened to them. No one's going to believe Columbus just fell off the end of the earth.

So let's be nice to Chris. He'll go back and explain that there are already people living here in America and we have a new policy: no illegal immigrants.

FRED WASHINGSON, DELEGATE TO THE CONGRESSIONAL CONGRESS REPRESENTING THE FOURTEENTH COLONY, FRED'S PLACE DOWN BY THE CREEK

Guys, I don't know about this Declaration of Independence that's so popular all of a sudden. If we split from the English, we'd lose more than we could possibly gain.

First, it's their language. What are we going to speak? I don't know a single person around here who can speak American. Do you?

And have you tried those muffins? They'd go great toasted with a little cream cheese, as soon as we invent cream cheese.

Plus, look at this trick I've been working on with this ball. I call it putting English on the ball. I tried putting American on it, but it didn't work. And I think it could really come in handy later on if we hang on to that English national pastime, baseball.

MILD BILL HIKKUP, 978TH FASTEST GUN IN THE WEST

Billy the Kid? Who are we kidding here? If he's a kid, I'm Sitting Bull. Anyone old enough to gun down people in the back, that's a man as far as I'm concerned.

And what's with Wyatt Earp? Did he get up on the wrong side of the saddlebag or what? I mean, it's supposed to be: Go water the horses at the OK Corral. Or rent a buggy at the OK Corral. No one goes there for a gunfight. You want to shoot it out, isn't that what we have saloons for?

It's like I told General Custer, "Next time you feel the urge to yell, 'Charge!' count first. What could it hurt? Basic rule of massacres, Cus—if there's more of them than there are of you, go back to the fort. Watch the grass grow. I think there's a good sunset on tonight. If you have some burning need to get taken by the Native Americans, wait until they open casinos. Enough slot machines and they're going to get back everything we stole from them."

LAUGHS FROM THE FUTURE

★ ★ ★ ★ ★ ★ ★ ★ ★ ★

Looking into our crystal ball, we see an awful lot of crystal in the future. Also, these future trends, which will make life better, or at least not much worse than it already is.

COMBO BOOKS

No time. To read.

Books. Too slow.

How to increase reading productivity?

At last there's help for the reading-challenged. Wouldn't your life be more efficient if you could read twice as many books in the same time as old-fashioned people read one book?

Now you can, through Combo Books. Everyone you know has two cars, two jobs, and two therapists. It's time to double your literary efficiency by reading two books at the same time. You'll enjoy these Combo Books twice as much:

Lake Wobegon Days of the Locust
The Old Man in the Gray Flannel Suit and the Sea
Romeo and Juliet and Franny and Zooey
101 Dalmatians Flew over the Cuckoo's Nest
Tender Is the Night of the Iguana
The Wings of the Lonesome Dove
War and a Separate Peace

HOLIDAYS THAT CELEBRATE THE ORDINARY THINGS

National Déjà Vu Day: Whatever you had for breakfast yesterday, have the same thing today. Wear the usual clothes. Go to the same old job. Come back home to the same old people. Oh wait, I guess we call that Tuesday.

National Yes But Day: The Thursday after Thanksgiving, when we consider all the things we would be even more thankful for if they had been done just a little bit better.

"Thank you, Lord, for the food you put on the table. But does the turkey have to be quite so dry? And those rolls—good, but not burned on the bottom would be even better. And while we're fixing things up, not having Uncle Phil over next year would give us that much more to be thankful for. So if we're going to count our blessings, is it okay if we count by twos?"

INVESTMENTS IN MENTAL HEALTH

Analysts tell us that if we work hard during analysis, we can turn our feeling of total misery and utter rejection into a common, ordinary unhappiness, and at quite a bargain price.

It now costs $150 a fifty-minute hour to find out why you're feeling so bad. It used to cost a lot less, but there's been an inflation in depression.

There's also a recession in schizophrenia, but no one believes it's actually happening.

On the whole, it looks like the investment potential for psychoanalysis will remain strong through the first quarter, unless there's a sudden downturn in the market, in which case smart neurotics will get out of analysis and into prayer.

BONUS CHAPTER 5

ODD THOUGHTS

★ ★ ★ ★ ★ ★

For many of us, all we have are odd thoughts. But if you've looked in the cupboard and found a bear, then here are a few from my personal supply of Odd Thoughts that you can borrow.

HOW NOT TO CATCH FLIES

Business consultants tell companies to offer their customers incentives for doing the right thing, instead of punishing them with extra fees for doing it wrong.

"Here's a discount for booking early." Rather than "You've booked late. We have to charge you with the ITTGOOTOETAC fee." That stands for: I'm Trying to Get Out of the Office Early Today Annoying Customer fee.

"You'll catch more flies with honey than with vinegar," the consultants wisely point out, right before they send the company a large bill for wisdom allocation.

What the consultants never tell you is: What are you going to do with all those extra flies?

Frankly, I've spent a lot of time trying to get rid of flies. So hold the honey. Pass the vinegar.

WHY WE SHOULDN'T JOIN IN

You ever go to a show where the performer asks you to sing along? "Come on everybody, join in!"

Or they do that over-the-head clapping demo so you'll clap along as they sing and provide the rhythm section so the drummer can take a break. Or they ask you to cheer for your city.

Happens just about every single show, doesn't it? Except maybe the opera.

You're a good person, so you join in, and so does everyone else in the audience. Now you're paying to hear yourself perform, which you could do for free in the shower. Meanwhile, the person getting all the ticket money for the show is just goofing on the stage, watching you.

Let's say you and a thousand other good people have just shouted out, "Chicago!" Or sung, "Rock, rock, rock, rockin' robin."

Then ninety-nine times out of a hundred, the performer with control of the mike will say the exact same thing: "I can't hear you." And you have to do it all over again.

What is it with the performers' union? Apparently, they only hire the hard of hearing.

Why are audiences obligated to prove their worthiness to the performers? Shouldn't it be the other way around? Isn't it more important for the audience to hear the performers? If they want to hear us so badly, give us the mike.

Didn't we just pay $79.80 apiece for the privilege of having you do the show? Are your ticket prices so low that we have to subsidize you by putting on this cooperative performance?

You can't hear us? Listen harder. We're all out here shouting about something.

WHY WE'RE A WORLD OF PEOPLE WHO CHOOSE (C)

Religion tells us that we only think we're miserable. Apparently, we don't understand that human suffering is actually part of the plan. Misery is the way it's supposed to work. Oh.

The way I figure it, at some point during those first six days before God knocked off work, He had a choice among:

(a)   No suffering.
(b)   Some suffering just to keep our feet on the ground.
(c)   A lot of suffering with intermittent giddiness.
(d)   All suffering, all the time.

God, in His wisdom, chose (c). Or maybe God was like a lot of high school students who haven't done their homework and choose (c) under the when-you-don't-know-the-right-answer-choose-(c) theory because it comes up more often than a, b, or d.

Maybe He should have spent a little more time cracking the books when He took Design 101 back in God College. Just our luck to live in a world created by a B-minus god. Oh, well, maybe next time He'll get it right.

REALITY WORKS BETTER IN THEORY THAN IT DOES IN REALITY

As a society, we can't improve the actual quality of life for more than the top .01 percent of the people. But we can improve the perception of quality of life by making it more like TV commercials.

That's why so many commercials try to convince us we're dumb. It lowers the standard for everyone else.

If life was more like advertising, you would be home by now. You'd also be rich. And you'd be so beautiful that we would be over at your place whispering in your ear, because we would be beautiful too.

But life—with all its violent uncertainty and insufficient parking—is not an attractive buy. People develop their negative views of reality from the phenomenon sociologists call "what they see all around them."

Research shows that when people view life as pointless, they grow too depressed to shop. This doesn't slow down the corporations because people who think that life is nothing but a long stretch of boredom and misery, broken up by fleeting delusions, represent a tremendous marketing opportunity. Basically, it's everybody from the old market, but all over again.

WE SHOULD CANCEL THE NOBEL PEACE PRIZE UNTIL WE GET SOME ACTUAL PEACE

Cars get recalled when they prove defective (well, sometimes). So why shouldn't the Nobel Peace Prize be recalled? After all, how much peaceful-style peace have we ever had?

These days a national leader can win a peace prize just for suggesting in a memoir: "Maybe we shouldn't have blown up everyone after all. Blowing up 70 to 80 percent of them probably would have gotten the point across. Oh well, live and learn."

The Nobel Peace Prize I particularly want recalled is the one they gave in 1906 to the Permanent International Peace Bureau, of which nothing has been heard since. They just don't make permanence like they used to.